AF415952

Girl Psychos

Jenna Dickens

Published by Trellis Publishing, 2021.

While every precaution has been taken in the preparation of this book, the publisher assumes no responsibility for errors or omissions, or for damages resulting from the use of the information contained herein.

GIRL PSYCHOS

First edition. July 16, 2021.

Copyright © 2021 Jenna Dickens.

ISBN: 979-8224405671

Written by Jenna Dickens.

GIRL PSYCHOS

JENNA DICKENS

CATHERINE BIRNIE

Catherine Margaret Harrison was born on May 23rd, 1951. Her partner, David John Birnie, was born on February 16th, 1951 and died on October 7th, 2015 by way of suicide. The duo was famously known throughout Australia as: The Killer Couple. They were from Perth, Australia and were found to have murdered four women ranging in age from 15 to 31 years old, over a span of about five weeks. Their fifth victim managed to escape through the bedroom window, while Catherine was distracted by a knock at the front door. The woman immediately ran and found help. The press referred to the heinous murders as the Moorhouse Murders. The victims were taken to Catherine and David's home located at 3 Moorhouse Street in Willagee, in Western Australia, a suburb of Perth.

Catherine was only two years old when her mother died in childbirth while giving birth to

Catherine's younger brother. Her brother also died, two days later. Catherine's father, Harold, couldn't manage raising Catherine on his own at that time so she went to live with her maternal grandparents. When she was ten years old, Harold petitioned the court to receive custody of Catherine again, and he won. There always seemed to be a battle. Catherine's father didn't want her, but then wanted her, always back and forth. After Catherine was convicted of four counts of murder, it caused her father to suffer a nervous breakdown.

When Catherine was twelve years old she met a boy named David Birnie and they began dating two years later when they became teenagers. Both Catherine and David came from dysfunctional families. Their home life was chaotic and messy, literally as well as figuratively. David's mother was an alcoholic and his father was away at work the majority of the time. His father died in 1986 after battling a long illness. The house, as well as his mother, were messy and unkempt. She left her older children in charge of taking care of their younger siblings. She refused to do anything when it concerned the children and their welfare. Allegedly, David's mother would leave the refrigerator door open so that the children could eat throughout the day. David was the oldest of five children. David's school friends, as well as the local priest, deemed the family dysfunctional. The parents never prepared meals for their children, the house was always a mess, and the Priest, before marrying David's parents, said that he felt that their marriage would never lead to anything good. Little did he know how accurate his assumptions would be.

Catherine and David met through mutual friends shortly after David's family moved to the same Perth neighborhood as Catherine and her father. Catherine's father felt that David was trouble and a bad influence. Catherine had begun getting into a lot of trouble with the local police ever since the two of them met. Harold begged and pleaded with Catherine to stay away from David and stay out of trouble. Of course, this just brought the two closer. Whenever two kids are told not to do something, they go out of their way to blatantly disobey.

Even in adolescence David began exhibiting violent and perverse behavior. When David turned fifteen he dropped out of school and began working as jockey apprentice for Eric Parnham at the Ascot Race Course. While there, David would hurt the horses and also began his perverse career as an exhibitionist. David committed his first rape shortly after. By this point he had spent time in and out of jail for several charges ranging from misdemeanors to felonies. He built up a reputation around town as a sex and pornography addict.

Catherine was an accessory to a lot of crimes because of her involvement with David. They built up an extensive history of numerous charges including: breaking and entering, trespassing, unlawfully driving a motor vehicle, and theft. Catherine took the time, while in jail, to decide it was time to get away from David and start over. David had to serve a long jail sentence, while Catherine got off with probation. With the help of her parole officer, she found a job as a housekeeper working for the McLaughlin family. She ended up marrying the families' oldest son, Donald McLaughlin, on her twenty first birthday. They went on to have seven children. One of her children, however, was killed in a car accident while he was only an infant, leaving her with six of her children to take care of. Catherine was never really interested in motherhood though, and wasn't proud of her children and her family like another mother might be. She wasn't concerned about the children or keeping up with the house. Catherine was never truly happy. Her thoughts kept going back to her childhood love, David Birnie. The family that she had left never saw Catherine as a violent or evil person. Not unless she was around David.

Catherine finally reconnected with David Birnie after a thirteen year separation, four weeks after she gave birth to their seventh child. David had escaped from prison and the two of them had begun seeing each other. Catherine left her family and everything behind when David popped back into her life. They finally moved in together and Catherine had her last name changed to Birnie, although the couple never formally or legally got married. They moved into a white brick, two bedroom bungalow on Moorhouse Street. The house was unkempt, the property looked untended, and the house needed a fresh coat of paint. Catherine was completely dependent on David, emotionally and physically. Catherine was easily controlled and manipulated by David, and she would do anything and everything to make him happy. She never wanted to disappoint him. David had an insatiable sexual appetite and was said to have sex up to six times a day. He also accrued an extensive pornography collection and his brother claimed he always had someone. He always had a woman around. David's brother, James, had ended up staying with Catherine and David for a short while. James had just recently been released from prison after serving time for his own sex related offenses. He stayed with the couple for about six months. His brother went on to describe the numbing spray that David would spray on his penis before he had sex with all of the different women.

David and Catherine had exhausted all of their options sexually and began looking for new ways to pleasure themselves. They had spoken about abduction and rape, but had not realized that it would be just a few short weeks before they turned their fantasies into a heinous and perverted reality. Being as emotionally dependent on David as she was, it was easy for David to talk her into his abduction and rape plans. Catherine could never tell him no. She felt that she couldn't survive without him and would do anything to keep him. Catherine was completely codependent and David always seemed to be in control. She wanted David to have all the pleasure and excitement that he wanted but knew that they had exhausted all efforts between just the two of them.

The abductions, rapes, and brutal murders began on October 6th, 1986. The couple didn't really care who their victims were, as long as they were female and alone. Twenty two year old Mary Neilson arrived at the Moorhouse Street residence to inquire about some tires that David had for sale. Mary was a student at the University of Western Australia where she was pursuing her degree in Psychology. Once inside the house, David took Mary by knife point and chained her to their bed and gagged her. Catherine stood in the room and watched as David raped the girl repeatedly. After the rape, the couple took Mary to Gleneagles National Park. David raped her one more time and then strangled her with a nylon cord and stabbed her through the heart. The couple then buried Mary in a shallow grave. Catherine looked on while David committed these violent acts, however, she did not yet participate.

The second murder took place on October 20th. The victim was fifteen year old, Susannah Candy. Susannah was a high school student attending Hollywood High School. She lived with her parents and had two brothers and one sister. Catherine and David Birnie had been driving around for several hours that night in search of their next victim. The couple finally found a girl walking along Stirling Highway, by herself, trying to hitch a ride. As soon as she got into David's car she had a knife to her throat and she was taken to the Birnies' home. While at the home, she was forced to write letters to her family explaining that she decided to run away. David repeatedly raped Susannah while she lay bound and gagged. Catherine had gotten into the bed with them and tried to strangle her with the nylon cord, but Susannah began fighting back. They forced sleeping pills down her throat, and once she passed out they successfully strangled her with the cord. The couple took Susannah to the State Park and buried her in a shallow grave, like their previous victims. This was the first time that Catherine took part in the murder. Catherine never showed any form of remorse over what she had done. When later asked why she contributed she said, "I wanted to see how strong I was within my inner self. I didn't feel a thing. It was like I expected. I was prepared to follow him to the end of the earth and do anything to see that his desires were satisfied. She was a female. Females hurt and destroy males."

On November 1st, the Killer Couple comes across their third victim, Noelene Patterson. Noelene was on her way home from work when her car ran out of gas. Noelene was a bar manager and had been working at Nedland's Golf Club that day. She was standing beside her car when David pulled up to her and offered his help. The thirty one year old got into David's car and was immediately met with a knife at her throat. She was taken to Moorhouse Street where she was bound and gagged, while being raped repeatedly. The original plan, like the others, was to kill the girl that same night. David had seemed to develop feelings for Noelene however. Catherine noticed the fondness that David had for the woman and became extremely jealous and increasingly upset. Noelene represented the type of person that Catherine could only wish to be and she absolutely despised her because of this. Catherine gave David an ultimatum at this point. She put the knife to her own chest and said, 'you either kill her tonight, or I will kill myself.' It was on the third night, after being given the ultimatum, that David gave Noelene several sleeping pills and then strangled her. She was then taken to the park and buried beside the other victims. Catherine admitted to taking pleasure in throwing sand in the victims face as David coldly buried her with no remorse.

Catherine and David's fourth victim, Denise Brown, suffered the same fate as the previous women who had the unfortunate experience of crossing paths with the Killer Couple. Denise Brown was twenty one years old, and was taken on November 5, 1986 while waiting at a bus stop. She was gagged and raped repeatedly before being put into the car and taken to Pine Plantation, where she was raped again while David waited for a blanket of darkness to fall. After it got dark he took her out and raped her again, while stabbing her in the neck. As David began burying her, thinking she was dead, Denise surprised the couple by sitting straight up in her grave. David struck her in the head twice with an axe as Catherine looked on in shock and amazement. David has said that he learned bodies would decompose at a faster rate if you stabbed them.

Detective Sergeant Paul Ferguson was the first to realize that he could be dealing with a serial killer, after the fourth woman was reported missing. Years later he recalled his experience while working on the case. He recalls how this case still haunts him and when asked why replied, "Because it was the most interesting and horrific I've had in my career," and "I have things tucked away back here that I pray to God I never pull out of the drawer." All of the missing women had come from relatively good homes and they never got into any real trouble. Their families found the phone calls and letters they received very suspicious.

The couples' fifth and final victim was seventeen year old Kate Moir. She was on her way home, after a night out with her friends, when she was abducted by the couple. The date of this final abduction was November 10th, 1986. Kate was the only one of their victims that was able to escape and run and find help. David had left the house for work that day. Catherine was home with Kate. She forced her to call her parents and tell them that she would be staying at a friend's house. When Catherine heard a knock at the door, she left Kate alone, untied, and went to see who was there. Kate took the opportunity to escape through the open window and ran half naked to the nearest store. She ran in crying and pleading for help. Kate was taken to the Palmyra police station and questioned. She was able to give the police a full description of Catherine and David, as well as inform the police of the couples' address. After their arrest, Catherine admitted to knowing Kate, but the couple said that the sexual acts were consensual and she was a willing participant. The police performed a search of the Birnie's home and found Kate's bag, as well as a pack of cigarettes that Kate had managed to hide in the ceiling in order to prove that she was there. After hours of questioning, Catherine and David finally admitted to the rape and murders of the four women and agreed to show the police where they had buried them. Three of the victims had been buried in Gleneagle State Forest and one on the Pine Plantation. The couple showed no emotion, whatsoever, as the police dug up the graves. David was the one who showed the police the locations of the women, except for one. Catherine insisted that she be the one to show them where Noelene was buried. She showed no regret, only anger. She spat on Noelene's grave and made her strong feelings of hate toward her very vocal to the detective. She explained to the police, in great detail, how much she despised Noelene Patterson. As they were leaving, David turned to Detective Katich and said chillingly, "What a pointless loss of young life." They showed absolutely no remorse for what they had done. This statement stuck with the detectives for years to follow. They couldn't believe how little the couple seemed to care or regret what they had been done. In some ways, however, they thought Catherine was relieved that it was finally over.

Catherine admitted to not caring about participating in the rapes and murders of the women, until they got to Denise Brown. "I think I must have come to a decision that sooner or later there had to be an end to the rampage. I had reached the stage when I didn't know what to do. I suppose I came to a decision that I was prepared to give her a chance." The brutal manner in which Denise was murdered seemed to hit Catherine hard. She witnessed David not only stab her repeatedly but strike her in the head with the axe. "Deep and dark in the back of my mind was yet another fear. I had a great fear that I would have to look at another killing like that of Denise Brown, the girl he murdered with the axe."

In response to Kate Moir's escape, due to Catherine's carelessness with her victim, she said, "I knew that it was a foregone conclusion that David would kill her, and probably do it that night. I was just fed up with the killings.

I thought if something did not happen soon it would simply go on and on and never end."

Kate Moir survived the abduction and attacks of Australia's most infamous serial killers. Instead of remaining a victim, she chose to be a survivor. She also sought to seek reform for the way her government handled cases like hers.

"I want to see no parole for wilful murder. I want a reintroduction of wilful murder as a charge. I want truth in sentencing. I want no parole for sex offenders and child sex offenders. We have been softening our justice system for years."

Kate Moir is a married woman and mother of three children. She constantly fights for the changes and justice she deserves. The following are quotes that were made by Kate, again concerning Catherine's parole and the possibility of her release.

"I want the legacy that I leave to be that of a survivor and a hero, not a victim. But enough is enough."

"I want the Attorney General to change the law and stop reviewing Catherine Birnie's parole. She does not apply for it herself, it is automatically reviewed and every time it happens, it causes me incredible pain."

"Every time I hear that her parole is being reviewed, I relive the nightmare. It causes significant trauma because I relive it and it feels like it happened yesterday. My name was always protected because I was a minor at the time I was captured, but due to the internet, if anybody googles my name it is everywhere and linked to the Birnie killings."

The couple appeared in court on November 12th, 1986. This was just two days after their fifth victim had escaped and they were arrested. The court proceedings took place at Fremantle Magistrates Court. They both refused any kind of representation, no plea was entered, bail was refused, and they were remanded into custody. Catherine allegedly took photos and the couple also recorded video of their criminal acts. At trial, the police were in possession of the video evidence. On February 10, 1987 a crowd gathered outside of the courthouse. When they saw the couple being ushered in for trial they screamed and chanted, "Hang the Bastards!" The community was outraged over the news of the serial killings that took place and wanted David and Catherine to receive the maximum sentence. They even wanted to reinstate the death penalty for David and Catherine Birnie.

Bill Power, the court reporter, spoke about the proceedings and the manners in which the couple acted while in court. He said that it would be something that would always stick with him, he would never forget.

"There was nothing distinctive about David and Catherine when they first appeared in court to face multiple murder charges in the serial killings which brought an end to the mystery of young women going missing off Perth streets."

"They were a rather nondescript, ordinary looking couple you might find running a petrol station in a country town. David was a weedy little man and Catherine his drab, slightly buxom wife with a very sour face. Both were accompanied by male police officers."

"If you have ever witnessed a wild cat go off, then try and imagine some hellcat in the confined spaces of a narrow staircase. Catherine Birnie fought against the guarding police officers and refused to allow any of them to touch her as she screamed and spat her words at them until she reached the dock and spotted her beloved, David. Only then did she calm down."

It had also been said previously, by some people in the community that the couple never looked like the type that could commit such violent acts. They looked like normal and ordinary people. But the secret horrors of what occurred in their home on Moorhouse Street would paint a very different image of the couple.

Trial Judge Justice Wallace said in trial, "Each of these horrible crimes were premeditated, planned, and carried out cruelly and relentlessly over a comparatively short period."

Right before Judge Wallace sentenced Catherine, he delivered the following message to her. He explained that he did not believe that even though she pled guilty, that she was truly sorry for what she had done. She had pled guilty and avoided a long trial, and spared the victims' families from having to relive over and over what happened to their loved ones, but she showed no remorse, no emotion, no sympathy for the crimes she had committed with David Birnie.

"You willingly joined in the selection of your unfortunate victims, carried them off at knifepoint, and held them in captivity for the sole purpose of the sexual gratification of your partner in crime and then murdered them, lest you be identified, and then finally mutilated them. You personally extinguished the life of two of your victims and certainly participated in the death of the third. The only appropriate punishment is the sentence I intend to impose, strict life security in prison."

Remember, Catherine was completely devoted, obsessed, and brainwashed when it came to David. She would do anything and everything for him to make sure he was happy. This is the driving factor that David used to manipulate and control her. He needed an accomplice and she was more than willing, and he knew it. Catherine and David received four separate life sentences for the abduction, torture, rape, and murder of Mary Neilson, Susannah Candy, Noelene Patterson, and Denise Brown. Under sentencing laws, their case was brought up every three years automatically for parole. Kate began a crusade to ensure that the couple remained in prison. She grew a social media presence and page entitled, We Support Kate, as well as worked with the Empowerment Foundation in an attempt to build an online reform petition. Kate also received support from Catherine's son, Peter. He chose not to release his surname to the public, due to the physical and emotional abuse he has been forced to face in relation to his mother's crimes. He had suffered personal and professional ruin, as soon as people learned about his family history. He had been turned down for jobs, lost jobs he had, and even lost his fiancé because of his family background. Peter was only five years old when his mother was arrested. He saw his mother on television because of it shortly after her arrest. When speaking out on the abuse he faced, he recalled horrible stories of what happened to him, and his siblings, while growing up. He also stated that the mandatory parole hearings, every three years, prevented him from getting on with his life. Having to hear about his mother and relive the violence his mother was responsible for every few years, was an interruption to his life, and it made it harder to maintain a sense of normalcy within his career life and personal life. In an interview with the West Australian, Peter stated, "I want the parole board to hear I don't want her out. I don't want to see her out." He also said, "I have had baseball bats to the head, I have been jumped on and kicked at. I have been knocked out."

After pleading guilty and receiving their sentences, David was initially sent to maximum security Fremantle Prison, he was eventually moved into solitary confinement. He did not get along with the other prisoners and was constantly getting into fights. The inmates frequently and violently attacked David. A day before he was due in trial for the charge of rape of an inmate, David hung himself in his jail cell. His suicide occurred in 2009 at Casuarina Prison. Catherine's request to attend David's funeral was refused.

Catherine was sent to Bandyup Women's prison where she was eventually employed as the head librarian. While in prison, the couple exchanged over 2600 letters, but were denied any other form of contact. Catherine's mandatory parole hearings were finally revoked in 2009, and her papers were subsequently marked: 'never to be released.'

While many people are against Catherine Birnie ever getting parole, one man stands against this argument. Perth QC Tom Percy disagrees with the opinion of people that had been saying that some people just don't deserve a second chance. The following quotes by Percy outline his argument of Catherine not remaining in prison and the likelihood of her harming the community, as well as his stance of being in favor of Catherine's parole.

"She should not be kept in prison to satisfy society's thirst for revenge."

"She has been there thirty odd years and you would think it might be time for us to say she has done her time. She has done her statutory minimum prescribed by the court, which was in possession of all of the facts."

"I am not sure she could really be a threat to anyone anymore, and all my information from Bandyup Womens' Prison is that she is a little old granny that goes about her work in the library like a church mouse."

"This case just so happened to be one that caught the public attention, even though she was not the prime mover in it. David is now dead."

"What's the point of keeping her in there? Sadly, it looks like she will never get parole, but I think she probably deserves it."

Despite his argument and fight to get Catherine released from prison, she still remains behind bars. She has not requested any new parole hearings, herself, as of yet. Some people in the community had gone as far as to say that if she were to be released, then maybe Percy should allow her to live with him in his residence.

It was now January of 1987. A letter written by Catherine Birnie, while in prison, eventually surfaced. It was a letter she had written to her six children in an attempt to explain some of her actions that led to her being placed in prison and why she left them in the first place. The letter reads as followed:

"Dear kids, Hi! Mum here...the reason I changed my name to Birnie was so that you kids wouldn't be hurt by the newspapers and television people. I am not proud of what has been said about me, but I have to live with that and the memories. As to why this happened, I can only hope that the doctors can help me to find out.....I never stopped loving any of you kids. Maybe I was wrong about leaving you but I thought you would be safer with your father."

Catherine's husband, Donald, claimed that he had still wanted her back. This was after trial and after he heard of the horrific acts she had committed with David. He stated, 'you can't stop loving someone after fifteen years of marriage.' Donald's mother stood firmly beside her son, saying that Catherine had been good and non-violent, until David cast his spell over her. Catherine's nephew, Leonard Nock, stood beside his aunt claiming, "All Aunt Cathy wanted was someone to lean on. She never had a mother. She is a very caring person. She and I are very close. I used to call her my mum. She was never the violent type, she never used to hit the kids. It is not the Cathy we used to know and love." In Catherine's letter she also persuaded the children to tell their father to divorce her. She said their father needed to move on and this was the way it needed to be done. She didn't hold out any hope for her eventual release and didn't want Donald to wait for her, because it was never going to happen. She also asked the children to get permission from Donald to write back to her, and maybe even one day go and visit her. The family put the entirety of the blame on David. They refused to admit to or believe that Catherine had anything to do with the violence. During their prison visits, the family also failed to even ask Catherine the question regarding her guilt or innocence. They didn't want to hear the answer, therefore, they never even asked the question.

Catherine Bernie was up for parole in 2013 and again in 2016. She was denied both years. She is once again up for review sometime in 2019. "Now barring any reason to keep her in, and revenge I don't consider enough of a reason. She should be released."-Percy

Despite Percy's statements, Catherine Birnie remains in prison to this very day, with little to no chance of parole. People, even to this day, wonder if the abductions, the perverse rape, and heinous murders would have continued long past the few weeks they had gotten away with it. If they had never been caught, would they have continued? Finally, were there other victims that they never confessed to? Other gravesites that have yet to be located? It is too late for David Birnie to tell anyone, but Catherine still has the chance to admit to any other wrongdoing she had done before her permanent home in prison forced her to keep distance between herself and her lover. I guess we will never know.

"I honestly believe that woman has never given those victims one ounce of consideration, both the dead victims and the families of the victims...They [David and Catherine Birnie] were parasites who lived off of each other. The most evil people I have ever, ever come across."-Detective Paul Ferguson.

THE VALENTINES DAY MURDER
ANA BENSON

Richard and Stacy Schoeck had a perfect marriage, or at least it looked ideal for their friends and family. Even though they have been together for a long time, they seemed to have eyes only for each other. Richard was Stacy's fifth husband and everyone was certain that he was indeed the love of her life. The couple still went on dates and celebrated their love in every way possible. So when Valentine's Day in 2010 came around, the Schoecks were setting up a romantic little getaway and a card exchange in a picturesque Belton Bridge Park which is located in Lula, Georgia.

Lula is a quiet little tourist town so when their Police Department received a frantic phone call with Stacy on the other end of the line, they knew something serious had happened. The town was shocked to discover that a murder occurred right there in their calm little oasis. But soon enough, the sinister plot started to unravel and the law enforcement realized that things were not as they seemed.

So what made Stacy Schoeck turn on her loving husband and who helped her with the murderous plan?

Early life

Stacy Morgan was born in 1971 in Florida. Her childhood wasn't perfect at all and her father died when she was really young. This left a permanent mark on Stacy even though her mother remarried soon and she did have a father figure in her life. She was also molested during this time frame by an individual who remained anonymous to everyone around her. Stacy grew up to be a lovely teenage girl who would fall in love easily. She met her first husband while she was still in high school and the couple got married shortly after. Unfortunately, he wasn't what Stacy was looking for and it took her two years to come to this conclusion. She filed for a divorce and the two separated.

When Stacy was twenty years old, she met her second husband. Soon after the wedding, Stacy found out that she was pregnant with her first child. The marriage lasted a little more than a year and she once again filed for a divorce when her son was just a toddler. Instead of being beaten down by two failed marriages, Stacy remained strong and made a decision to improve herself. After all, she was only twenty-two years old. She applied for college and got accepted. Stacy moved on to raise her son on her own and earn a degree in psychology and nursing at the same time.

She managed to find the employment as soon as she got out of college. Stacy was still very optimistic about her love life and wanted to find someone to spend the rest of her life with. She met her third husband in 1997 but unfortunately, the marriage was short-lived once again. It lasted for only six weeks. Stacy decided to date casually in the future and gave birth to her second son in 1998. She was still a single mother but this didn't seem to bother her at all.

Stacy did need to improve her financial status and she found a better job opportunity at a clinic which was located in Atlanta. The family moved over there and she was ready to start over. She got an excellent position at the hospital's administration with the possibility of even better promotion. She would assist the doctors on a daily basis with various tasks. Stacy was a successful and independent woman who was capable of taking care of her two small boys on her own.

But something was still missing and Stacy was longing for a partner who would be there for her. She was tired of casual encounters and needed some stability. So in 2001 she married for the fourth time and moved out to a small town near Atlanta. She got pregnant once again and gave birth to her third son. She lived in a large house with her fourth husband and it seemed that her life was absolutely perfect. Her boys were happy and they loved the suburban lifestyle. On the other hand, Stacy was still unhappy. Soon after the separation from her fourth husband in 2005, Stacy met Richard Schoeck, a graphic designer who was slightly older than her. He was a patient at the hospital where Stacy worked at the time. The two hit it off immediately.

Richard Schoeck was an adventurer who lived his life to the maximum. Stacy was immediately attracted to his positive attitude and passionate outlook. Richard accepted Stacy's sons like they were his own and would often organize family outings that included the entire family. She loved how different Richard was from all of her previous husbands and thought that she had finally found the one.

Unconcerned about Stacy's previous failed marriages, Richard still wanted to make their relationship permanent. The couple did get married in 2007 but the ceremony wasn't standard at all. Stacy and Richard eloped and told everyone about the wedding once they came back home. It was in Richard's nature to do something so spontaneous and Stacy adored him for that.

Richard became a stay at home dad after the wedding and he would form a close bond with Stacy's boys. He was very involved with their school and hobbies so he ended up adopting the youngest two. He really did accept this small family as his own and wanted the best for the boys. Everyone approved of Richard and Stacy's family hoped that she finally found the man of her life. Unfortunately, this marriage would end up tragically in just a couple of years.

The murder of Richard Schoeck

Prior to Valentine's Day in February of 2010, Stacy invited Richard on a small romantic getaway to the town of Lulu, Georgia. They were supposed to meet in Belton Bridge Park which is a secluded area near the town itself and exchange gifts there. This wasn't unusual for the Schoecks because they would often go on different adventures that were supposed to spice up their love life. The Police dispatchers received a frantic phone call sometime after the nightfall. Stacy was screaming that her husband was shot and robbed. He wasn't showing any signs of life.

The police arrived at the scene of the crime and sure enough, Richard's body was lying next to his pickup truck. The blood was both inside and outside of the vehicle which meant that several shots were fired. At least one bullet hit him while he was still in the driver's seat or getting out of the car. He crawled out, perhaps to run away or defend himself. The shooter continued firing the gun until they were certain that Richard was dead.

The investigators immediately closed off the area and examined the tire tracks which were visible in the surrounding mud. They noticed that the third vehicle was definitely there and that it left the scene of the crime prior to the arrival of Stacy. The law enforcement marked them as the evidence. However, there were some red flags that indicated that this wasn't a standard robbery. For instance, Richard's valet was still in the car and his jewelry was on him. Nothing was taken from the scene.

Stacy wasn't a suspect at the time but the police escorted her to the station in order to interview her and get as many details as possible. Lulu is a quiet town where crime rarely happens so the law enforcement couldn't zero in on any possible reason why Richard was shot. One theory suggested that he might have interrupted another couple at Belton Bridge Park because it was a common meeting ground for lovebirds who wanted to spend some time together outside of their homes.

The interviews and investigation

Once Stacy got to the station, she started talking. She was asked to explain what they were doing at the remote park and she admitted that they did have problems in their marriage. She thought this would be the perfect time to add some flare to their relationship. Since Richard was a stay at home dad and she had difficult work hours, the two simply couldn't get any alone time to spend with each other. She was becoming desperate and unhappy.

She quickly admitted to having an affair to the shock of everyone who was present in the interrogation room. Her lover was a fellow co-worker from the hospital who was significantly younger than Richard. His name was Juan and he was a complete opposite of Stacy's husband. She needed intimacy and she fell in love with someone else who could give her everything she craved for. Stacy even took her lover to Las Vegas just a couple of weeks prior to the murder of her husband.

The detectives were interested in the affair and started asking questions related to the possibility that Stacy wanted to get out of her marriage with Richard in order to be with her new man. Stacy told them that she did think about leaving Richard but that no particular plans were made. She knew how much her children loved him and getting a divorce would probably break their hearts. They focused on Stacy's lover but she quickly debunked their claims by saying that he is not violent at all and that she cannot imagine him being involved with anything involving guns or shooting.

But Stacy did say that Juan knew about the rendezvous in the park so the police decided to call him up for an interview the next morning. Juan seemed oblivious to the events that took place last night and he told the detectives that Stacy claimed her relationship with Richard was open. This meant that each of them had someone on the side. Juan didn't seem to be bothered by this arrangement at all so the investigators started doubting their possible theory. Plus, Juan had a solid alibi for the time of the murder because he was in another city.

They were left without any solid lead in this case so it was time to look a bit further and include as much aid as possible. The park is a fairly isolated place but there was a nearby cell phone tower that covered the entire area. The investigators knew that if a call was placed from that location on the night of the murder, they would have the number listed. And it turned out that this was a crucial move made by the investigators because it would lead them in the right direction.

The list of calls was short because that cell tower is not in an urban area. The detectives used the contact information which was stored in both Stacy's and Richard's phones and they tried to find the match. Stacy's phone had the number that was called sometime around the murder. The contact info itself stood out because it said Mr. Results. The investigators were slightly confused because they had no idea who this person was. But calling him up would probably shed some light on the events that occurred on Valentine's Day.

The police quickly identified the mystery man who was present at the scene of the crime that night. His name was Reginald Coleman and he worked as a private fitness instructor in Atlanta. Coleman was born in Philadelphia but his criminal past led him to move out from his hometown and try to start over in another state. He was incarcerated in the past but managed to clean up his act. Coleman was doing fine financially and owned a fairly popular gym. As far as the local police force knew, he was staying away from any type of crime.

Todd Woodten who would become Coleman's attorney during the trial said the following on his client: "Reginald was a true survivor. He was street-savvy and always had a hustle going on. He did a lot of things for youth, trying to keep them off the street and keep them safe."

Once the police managed to attain the call records from Reginald Coleman's cell phone, they found the number he had called from the Belton Bridge Park. The investigators thought they would see Stacy Schoeck's digits but they were surprised with their discovery. Coleman called another woman - Lynitra Ross. The detectives then realized that the whole plot was more complicated that they initially assumed and that there are more players involved with the murder of Richard Schoeck. So how did all of them fit together?

After speaking to Coleman's friends, the police found out that Lynitra Ross was his ex-girlfriend who would often resurface in his life. But there was another detail that connected Lynitra to the murder — she worked at the same hospital as Stacy Schoeck and two of them were really good friends. Stacy was Lynitra's boss and a landlord. Since there was a third set of tire marks on the scene of the murder, the detectives quickly determined that the model did not fit the tires on Reginald's car. This did sidetrack them a bit but they were still determined to find out what really happened.

The investigators were certain that they did, in fact, have their suspect and that was Stacy Schoeck. However, they still had to connect the dots so they dug even further into the phone records of those three. There was a message exchange on the night prior to the murder of Richard Schoeck between the three parties. However, the most interesting clue was Stacy's bank account which clearly stated that she sent a total of $10,000 to Lynitra's account which she passed along to Reginald.

The arrests

Since the topic of the third vehicle was still the big unknown, the police started going through all cars which were somehow related to Stacy, Lynitra, and Reginald. And soon enough they were onto something. Stacy did have one car which she sold soon after the murder. It wasn't registered to her but she did use it often in order to drive her relatives or get them groceries. They were surprised to find out that Stacy put their vehicle on the market but she told them that they will get a newer model as a gift from her.

The police became very suspicious of this story so they tracked down the new owner and took a look at the tires as well as the insides of the car. And yes, the tire marks matched perfectly. Stacy Schoeck borrowed that car to Reginald Coleman on that fatal Valentine's Day. The evidence against Coleman was piling up and he was arrested on May 25th, 2010. But as soon as the interrogation started, he denied any involvement with Stacy Schoeck or the murder of her husband.

Lynitra Ross was arrested a couple of hours after Reginald but she also refused to provide the investigators with any useful information. It was time to pick up Stacy as well so the police arrived at the medical center she worked at and led her straight to the station. The investigators had plenty of circumstantial evidence to accuse her of the murder and they didn't have to wait for her accomplices to start talking about the crime. All three of them were in custody and it was time to face the justice for their actions.

Psychological assessment

Stacy Schoeck was put through a psychological assessment prior to the trial itself in order to determine if she had any underlying problems which were unknown to her or her family. The murder was well planned so she clearly wasn't distraught at the time which meant that Stacy knew exactly what she was doing when she asked her friend Lynitra to help her get rid of her husband.

The psychologists took a closer look at her prior relationships and marriages which ended in divorce. The reason for her unhappiness might lay in the fact that she lost her biological father when she was young and she was unable to connect to anyone. Not to forget that Stacy was also molested when she was just a child.

It was obvious that Stacy Schoeck was manipulative and knew how to get exactly what she wanted in every situation. Her intelligence was obviously high because she did put herself through school and successfully earned her degrees. However, her actions towards Richard Schoeck show that Stacy was also a sociopath because she hired a man to murder her husband and continued to live her life as nothing happened.

She mourned her husband publicly and got very emotional in front of her friends and family every time they saw her. The fact that she selected Valentine's Day as the date of the execution speaks volumes about her cold-heartedness towards Richard Schoeck.

The trials of Ross and Coleman

The first of three to stand a trial was Lynitra Ross. She entered the courtroom in May 2012 and was facing charges for a murder. After all, she was a co-conspirator who helped Stacy Schoeck find the hitman who would eventually pull the trigger and take Richard's life. Stacy was also present in the courtroom but she wasn't the accused in this situation. As a matter of fact, she testified on the side of the prosecution.

Stacy Schoeck was cooperating with the law enforcement and made a deal regarding her sentencing. She did everything to avoid the death penalty and was ready to talk about the murder of her husband. It was clear that her deeds were out in the open and she said the following as she took the stand: "I'm going to testify truthfully for Richard. It's all I can give his mom and his family and the children — all I can give them is the truth."

The jury then heard the story about the murder plot. Stacy Schoeck had the idea to take her husband's life in December 2009 after she noticed that her boys were acting strangely. They were getting into troubles and she started to suspect that they might be victims of molestation. She remembered how she behaved during the time she was assaulted as a child and found the connection. Of course, her first suspect was Richard because he was always with the boys.

Stacy also said: "I was just so fixated in my mind that Richard was doing something wrong that I said, 'I don't want the cops, I don't want a divorce, I want him dead.'" She then admitted to asking an unnamed man to help her kill her husband but he stopped returning her calls. Then she talked to her friend and co-worker Lynitra Ross and told her about her suspicions. Lynitra responded with the suggestion that they talk to her ex-boyfriend who would know what to do because he was "an experienced hitman".

After Lynitra Ross contacted Coleman, the two woman drove to his house and sat down with him in order to agree on some finer details regarding the hit. They talked and ate food from Zaxby's. Stacy suggested the park as the perfect place for executing her husband because he wouldn't suspect a thing. Reginald and Stacy agreed on the amount of money she would pay him for the murder, as well as on the vehicle he would take to the park. All three of them went to Belton Bridge Park so that Stacy could show him the exact place where her husband will be waiting.

Stacy noted in her testimony the following: "The only times I ever saw or spoke to Reginald Coleman was the day we had Zaxby's that afternoon and the following Saturday when we went up to Belton

Bridge. Everything else was done through Lynitra." She also added that she had given Lynitra the property she was renting to her as the payment for the help.

Lynitra's defense lawyers took the stand and told the jury that Stacy's testimony which involved the molestation claims was slightly off due to the fact that she admitted to having an affair in the first interview she gave after the murder. She didn't mention anything related to the possible sexual abuse of her children.

In August of 2012, Lynitra Ross was sentenced to life in prison. There would be no possibility of a parole either. Even though she didn't pull the trigger, she was the person who set up Stacy and Reginald to meet. Therefore, she was directly involved in the murder plot.

It was later determined that Richard Schoeck didn't have anything to do with child molestation but Stacy's plan was already completed and her husband was dead. The investigators took her claims seriously and talked to the middle boy who immediately said that he never accused Richard of anything. As a matter of fact, he never even talked to his mother about the alleged abuse. However, this didn't stop Stacy's attorneys from building their case around this.

Reginald Coleman's trial didn't last long because as soon as he appeared in front of the judge in November of 2012, he pleaded guilty to the murder of Richard Schoeck. He also faced charges for owning the firearm as a convicted felon. Stacy Schoeck was set to testify against him as well, which meant providing the courtroom with the full account of Reginald's actions.

Reginald Coleman agreed to kill Richard Schoeck after he heard the story of the alleged molestation directly from Stacy and Lynitra. Since he grew up in foster care, he often listened to the stories from his friends about their own abuse. Coleman thought that he could help the boys have a normal childhood by eliminating the threat from their life. He pleaded guilty in order to avoid the death penalty which was already on the table if he went on a trial. Coleman received the punishment of life in prison without the possibility of a parole and some additional years for the possession of the firearm.

Stacy Schoeck's trial

Once Ross and Coleman received their sentences, it was time for Stacy to appear in court for her own trial. The proceedings began in December of 2012 at Hall County Courtroom. Since Stacy cooperated with the prosecution in the trials of Coleman and Ross, the death penalty was off the table. Judge Jason Deal listened to the witnesses who described Richard Schoeck as a loving father and an exceptional friend who would never harm anyone. Stacy's defense attorneys once again repeated the story of the alleged abuse and claimed that her actions were severe because she wanted to protect her children from the aggressor.

When Stacy took the stand, she admitted to the crime and asked the judge to give her mercy. The defense told the courtroom about Stacy's own abuse and that she was acting erratically. However, the fact that the murder was planned months before it happened painted a picture of someone who wanted to eliminate her husband. Stacy had plenty of time to make sure that Richard was really the abuser and contact the law enforcement but she failed to do so.

Stacy's lawyers asked Judge Deal to consider giving Stacy a possibility of a parole and to keep in mind her troubled past. They also pointed out that Stacy was behaving well in prison and that she deserves a second chance. However, she received the punishment of life in prison without a chance to get out after serving thirty years which was the primary goal of her defense team.

Attorney Lee Darragh who led the prosecution said: "Judge Jason Deal appropriately recognized that Stacey Schoeck was the engine that put this train in motion, until the death of her husband. Without her involvement, this would not have occurred." The courtroom was filled with emotions because a large number of Richard's friends showed up for the hearing. One of the saddest moments was when Stacy's mother read a note which was written by her youngest boy which said: "I miss her every hour of every day, just like Daddy Richard."

Initially, Stacy Schoeck and Lynitra Ross were placed in two separate prisons in order to avoid any possible conflicts between the two but they were soon moved to the same facility – Pulaski State Prison. Stacy's family was left to wonder what was really the reason for this heinous crime because the exact motive was never uncovered. They got the custody of Stacy's three sons.

CELESTE BEARD

47

JACKIE STONE

"She is really in my mind, a really despicable human being." - crime writer Diane Fanning

Millionaire executive Steven Beard woke up screaming.

Experiencing excruciating pain, he reached down and clutched his stomach. He felt the blood on his hands and panicked. His internal organs were oozing outside his belly.

Beard reached over and called for an ambulance. The paramedics worked in vain to stem his bleeding. The seventy-four-year-old writhed in pain but out of the corner of his eye, he saw his wife Celeste enter the room.

"Oh my God," Celeste said. "Steve! What happened?"

The medics pushed the woman back, not wanting her to interfere in his care.

Chaos ensued as his thirty-seven-year-old wife and her two twin daughters entered the room. Police searched around the premise and found a shell on the ground.

Steven Beard had been shot in his stomach.

But by whom?

Was it the wife who strangely was not sleeping in the same bed. The daughters?

Or would it be Tracey Tarlton, a lesbian lover of Celeste?

"They knew Tracey had pulled the trigger," crime writer Diane Fanning said. "But they suspected someone else was involved. But Tracey just wouldn't talk."

Tarlton harbored a secret from the police. She had fallen in love with Beard's wife, Celeste.

But as Tracey would later find out, there was a lot about Celeste that she didn't know about...

CHAPTER ONE

"Celeste Beard had a very rough childhood," Fanning said. "There was a lot of instability, alcoholic abuse in the family and she really had it rough."

The identity of Beard's biological parents has remained a mystery. She was one of four children raised by adoptive parents, Edwin and Nancy Johnson. Celeste would claim that both Edwin and one of her older adoptive brothers would sexually abuse her from age 4 to 12. Nancy, her adoptive mother, was psychologically unstable and be institutionalized on a regular basis.

On one occasion, Celeste's daughter Kristina would record a conversation she had with Celeste in which she talked about her sexual abuse.

"Do you know what it feels like when you're four years old, you aren't even in kindergarten? Do you know what that does to you?"

Celeste has maintained that both adoptive parents physically abused her when she was a child and that she had tried to kill herself during her early teens. At the age of seventeen, she married Craig Bratcher and gave birth to twins, Jennifer, and Kristina. The relationship with Bratcher was a volatile one, filled with physical assaults and restraining orders. The couple would divorce and Beard would lose custody of the twin daughters.

But Celeste could get men to marry her with ease. Easy come, easy go.

She would go on to marry Henry Wolfe, an Air Force mechanic. Once again, the relationship was tempestuous and Celeste would divorce. She would claim later that her own divorce lawyer gave her money to have a boob job done.

She would then move to Arizona and marry a man named Jimmy Martinez. Celeste had a gutter mouth and would spew vulgarities without any kind of filter. She would refer to Martinez' penis as the "BMW" (Big Mexican wiener) but the two would get divorced despite the alleged size of her husband's package.

By the time Celeste reached her mid-thirties, she was desperate for a better life. She worked as a waitress at the Austin Country Club.

"To use an old-fashioned term," Fanning said. "Celeste Beard was a fortune hunter and she was determined to make her way in the world on the back of someone else."

She would meet the wealthy Steven Beard at the Country Club, fawning over the elderly man as he dined with his wife, Elise.

"At the time, Steven was married to Elise," Fanning said. "And from what everyone was saying, they had a wonderful and happy marriage. Then Elise died of cancer and when that happened Celeste knew what she wanted."

She wanted a rich man.

Steven Beard would do.

CHAPTER TWO

Steven Beard was a self-made millionaire. He served in the Navy and went to college at both TCU and SMU. He started his career in radio advertising in Dallas, literally starting at the bottom. By the 1970s, he had graduated to television and in 1981 he had become the general manager of KBVO in Austin, Texas. Four years later, the station would become one of the first affiliates of the now behemoth Fox Network. The station grew by leaps and bounds and Beard would sell his share in the company which completed his fortune.

Celeste targeted the newly widowed Steven for his money. She preyed upon the loneliness and loss of the TV executive and he fell for her charm.

"She paid attention to him," Steven's daughter Becky Beard said. "That's what she needed at the time. That's what he needed the most was for someone to pay attention to him. And he just went hook, line, and sinker."

Three weeks after his wife died, Steven would take Celeste out on a date.

He took Celeste to Mama Mia's Italian restaurant then they had a nightcap at his mansion. The executive then allowed Celeste to borrow his $50,000 Lexus and drive herself home.

Steven spared no expense in his courtship probably figuring that the he could make up for the age difference between the two of them with money. He courted the thirty-eight years younger woman with an open checkbook which included a $16,000 diamond cocktail ring, a $3,000 wristwatch, and a new SUV.

But Steven's family, specifically his daughter, grew suspicious of Celeste's interest in her father.

"I think it was money," Becky said. "I think Celeste was after his money."

"Celeste was in dire straits," Orange said. "She had nothing but bad luck in life and men but always failed to see her own hand in her circumstance. With Steven, she had an older man who would overlook all of those things. He would be able to use his money to bail Celeste out of her debt, depression and dumb choices."

Steven had enough money to give Celeste a clean slate. Celeste had committed insurance fraud during her time in Arizona with Jimmy Martinez and had a $20,000 restitution bill that Steven ultimately paid for.

He then funded a renewed custody battle for Celeste's twin daughters. She would win the case and become reunited with Jennifer and Kristina. The couple did not inform the teen daughters of their union until later. Celeste would pretend to be Steven's housekeeper until one of her daughters caught the two in a hotel room during the 1993 Super Bowl.

The union did not have the blessing of Steven's family. They all thought she was marrying him for his money. Steven ignored their counsel and decided to marry Celeste. He was smart enough to have a prenuptial agreement drawn out. In the agreement, Celeste would receive over half-million dollars if they divorced but she would receive up to six million upon his death.

CHAPTER THREE

Celeste took immediate advantage of her newly acquired status as Mrs. Steven Beard. She went on a shopping spree after shopping spree, wildly spending money on whatever whims she could dream up.

"She was insane about spending money," Fanning said. "She could have gone a year and a half wearing a different pair of shoes and purse every day and not run out. At one point he gave her one million outright and she went through it in record time, like six months."

A part of the marriage agreement that Celeste didn't like was the fact that she had to play the role of a loving wife. She had no problem putting on appearances anywhere outside the bedroom. But in the bedroom was where the problem lay.

Celeste didn't want to have sex with Steven.

"She married him only for money," Fanning said. "So obviously she didn't find a seventy-five-year-old man attractive. So she really didn't want to be sexually involved with him."

On February 18th, 1995, Steven and Celeste would exchange vows at the Austin Country Club. Their honeymoon night involved a "sex needle" wherein Celeste had to insert a syringe into the base of Steven's penis in order for it to stiffen. She described the practice as "unromantic" and "kind of traumatizing."

In the months that followed, Steven wanted more sex than Celeste could put up with as she would refuse to inject the syringe into his penis. Feeling gypped, Steven would file for divorce four months after the wedding but changed his mind after Celeste came up with the "oral sex solution".

Sunday mornings would be reserved for pleasing Steven sexually, a day she referred to as the "Sunday Suck."

Celeste would do her wifely duties with great reluctance. She told her daughters that there should be no distractions at all during her Sunday morning time with Steven. She wanted to get things over with as fast as she could.

Things were going well for Steven. He was happy to have a hot, younger wife performing sex for him once a week.

That is, he was happy with the happy endings until he started to feel the financial burn.

Steven had given Celeste a $10,000 a month allowance but she thought of that as mere chicken feed. She had three walk-in closets that she lined with hundreds of pair of shoes, each with a purse to match. She would go on $50,000 shopping sprees and lavish her friends with gifts and parties. The couple would also take lavish vacations, on one occasion they visited China for a month where they spent over $100,000.

Steven started his marriage with over twelve million dollars in net worth. After only a year of marriage to Celeste, he was down to a rapidly dwindling eleven million.

Celeste would want more.

Much more.

CHAPTER FOUR

Celeste pressed Steven for even more money. She argued daily that the half-million prenuptial agreement was too low. She pressed Steven for more money and he would not budge. But Celeste would not let the issue go until one day Steven just relented. He wrote Celeste a check for a half-million dollars.

Six months later, Celeste had blown through the money.

Then she wanted more.

At that point, Steven blew up. He threatened to cut off all of her credit cards.

"Celeste told Steven that she was going to kill herself if Steven cut off her money supply," Orange said. "Shopping was like a drug for her. She had to have her daily fix. Just going to a mall to buy a pair of cheap shoes wouldn't do it for her. She had to have it all. Every day."

And now Steven no longer wanted to pay the price.

"She had to buy things in order to feel good," Orange said. "It wouldn't have mattered how much she purchased. It would have never been enough. Nothing would ever have been enough."

The final straw was the Christmas holidays of 1998. Celeste had spent nearly $300,000 dollars over a few weeks. Steven went ballistic and the shit started to hit the fan. Celeste grew more contemptuous of Steven as he questioned her spending. She often referred to him as "the fat bastard" or "the old fool."

"What the hell is that old man still doing alive?" she would cry out.

Celeste would start to act out even more. She would leave the mansion for long stretches and spend time at a weekend home that Steven owned along the river. She would not go there alone as she often entertained her ex-husband, Jimmy Martinez.

Steven would eventually find about her extra-marital trysts and threaten divorce.

This prompted Celeste to threaten suicide as a form of retaliation. She would be sent to a psychiatric facility called St. David.

There she would meet a woman named Tracey Tarlton.

Tracey was a manager at a trendy bookstore called the BookPeople. She was also an unstable mental patient who was looking for a girlfriend. One look at the glamorous Celeste was all it took for Tracey. She had to try her hand at seducing the heterosexual and married woman.

"Tracey was an emotionally unstable woman who had been in and out of hospitals for depression and other disorders for quite some time," Fanning said.

The two hit it off.

Tracey would claim that Celeste was "extremely flirtatious" with her in the beginning. She said that the two first had sex on March 20th, 1999 and that their relationship would continue until the day she would shoot Steven.

The two were not discreet about their romance. A photo of a company get together showed Celeste sitting on her lesbian lover's lap. People at the party would later report seeing the women kissing passionately.

Celeste was not a lesbian but she was willing to engage in a relationship with Tracey in order to get what she wanted. She admitted during an interview with a psychiatrist that she had to drink copious amounts of alcohol in order to prepare herself for sex with Tracey. Her daughters began seeing books about lesbian love around the house.

But while Celeste had to numb herself with alcohol, Tracey needed no such aids.

She was immediately smitten by Celeste and wrote her love letters just weeks after they met.

"Celeste, you are so beautiful," Tracey wrote. "I think about your long, silky body and your incredible, long legs and I just can't stand it. And then I think of your incredible face and I want to...stand outside your building and wait until I get arrested. We won't even talk about what happens when I think about your sweet, tough, sexy voice."

"Celeste had no problem trading sex for favors," Orange said. "So she used her sexuality in order to get Tracey to do her bidding."

And that bidding would be murder.

CHAPTER FIVE

When Celeste returned home, she could no longer hide her contempt for her husband. She would drug his drinks and then sneak out of the home to party with Tracey.

She couldn't just divorce the millionaire, however, as she had signed a pre-nuptial agreement.

"Because Celeste had signed a pre-nuptial agreement," Fanning said. "She was only guaranteed a minimum amount of money if she divorced Steven and he'd already given her that money and she'd blown it."

Celeste's daughters would catch their mother in bed with Tracey on occasion. Steven, always a step behind, would find out about Tracey just like he found out about Martinez. He would catch them sharing a lesbian kiss on the lips and would promptly chase Tracey out of the house.

Tracey feared for the future of their relationship after it became out in the open. She was in love with Celeste and fantasized about sharing a life together.

Celeste knew this and decided to use Tracey as a pawn.

Going into her best drama queen act, she tearfully told Tracey about how Steven would verbally abuse her on a daily basis. His constant belittling would leave her feeling suicidal.

"What are we going to do?" Tracey asked.

"I don't know," Celeste said. "Maybe we could kill him?"

"We?"

The idle talk soon turned serious as Tracey would do anything to keep Celeste in her life. Both women sat down and began discussing various ways of murdering Steven.

Their first idea was using a homemade botulism technique. They set some food aside, allowing it to spoil and rot. The two women then ground up the presumably poisonous substance and sprinkled it on a chili dog that the served to Steven.

Both of them watched in eager anticipation as Steven placed tainted food into his mouth.

"Jesus," Steven said as he munched on the hot dog. "This is delicious!"

After that attempt didn't so much as produce a tummy ache, the two women spiked Steven's Vodka with 190-proof alcohol (everclear).

The old man passed out and then they fastened a plastic bag around his head. The bag did not have the effect they wanted as he breathed just fine as he slept off the alcohol.

Feeling desperate, they decide to sprinkle grounded up sleeping pills and ecstasy tablets over his steak.

"Wow," Steven said as he chewed on the tender steak. "This is delicious!"

Nothing worked and the two inept killers became more desperate.

Celeste went into her drama queen act again. She told Tracey that she was dreading an upcoming trip to Europe.

"He's going to make me sleep with him," Celeste said in tearful disgust. "I just can't take it. I can't take it anymore."

"I want to help," Tracey said.

"Then do something!"

"Like what?"

"Kill him," Celeste said. "Kill him for me"

CHAPTER SIX

Tracey was willing to do anything for her lover. Celeste came over to her place and Tracey showed off her 20-gauge shotgun. Her father had given it to her as a gift and had her name engraved on the bottom.

"We can use this," Tracey said as Celeste looked the gun over in fake admiration.

"Tracey was there to do the bidding of Celeste," Orange said. "Celeste had all of the power in the relationship."

"Celeste planned the killing out very carefully," Fanning said. "She drugged her husband's drink to make sure he fell asleep. She went into the other wing of the house where she could justifiably say she heard nothing. Then she left the doors open so that Tracey could sneak in."

Tracey was more than a willing accomplice. She believed that once Steve was eliminated, she and Celeste could finally be together.

On October 2nd, 1999 Tracey stepped into the bedroom of the Beard home and shot Steven in his stomach.

"I had stepped into a space that was just numb when I went into that bedroom," Tracey recalled. "And I shot him."

Steven looked over and saw that his guts were literally, outside his stomach.

"911, what's your emergency?"

"I need an ambulance," Steven said in a pained voice. "Hurry."

"What's the emergency?"

"My guts just jumped out of my stomach. They blew out. Yeah, they blew out of my stomach. They're lying on my stomach."

"OK, they're lying on your stomach?"

"Yes, I'm in bed. I'm in awful pain. I'm having a hard time figuring out what happened. I don't know what happened. I've never had this happen before."

Steven was shell-shocked. He had slept through the gunshot but awakened to find himself with a hole in his stomach.

Deputy Alan Howard was the first to arrive at the Beard estate. He rang the doorbell and banged on the front door but received no answer.

Heard headed around toward the side window and saw Steven writhing in pain on the bed. He busted through the sliding glass and entered.

Sgt. Gregory Truitt arrived as well and the two officers thought that Steven had a surgical incision of some sort ripped open.

Two women then entered the bedroom, Celeste, and her daughter Kristina. A few minutes later, a deputy found a shotgun shell near the bed.

The medical emergency now had become a designated crime scene.

Police searched the home and found the bathroom ransacked. But they realized that the drawers that were ransacked "looked too deliberate."

"This wasn't a burglary gone bad," one of the deputies said. "It was a murder attempt staged to look like a break-in."

CHAPTER SEVEN

Tracey had performed the shooting in the belief that Celeste would do her part. Part of her job was to remove any and all evidence that Tracey was even there, one of which involved removing any shell casings.

But Celeste never picked up the shotgun shell.

She did keep quiet when the investigation ensued. Every family member and friend pointed to Tracey as a possible suspect except Celeste.

Police arrived at Tracey's home and asked if she had a gun. The woman agreed and the police requested that they test the rifle.

A ballistics match was made and Tracey would be arrested.

Steven would not die immediately from the gunshot wound.

His condition stabilized after seven surgeries. He would die four days after being released from the hospital as the wound become infected.

Celeste would remain by his side throughout his prolonged hospital stay.

But she also found time to shop, spending an astonishing $660,000 from October 1999 to March of 2000.

Steven would succumb from the wounds in January of 2000. Tracey Tarlton would be tried and convicted to life in prison for his murder.

True to her word, Tracey would remain silent in regards to Celeste's involvement.

But the police kept after her. They would try to reason with Tracey at first. When that didn't work, they would resort to taunting tactics.

"She really doesn't care about you," the police interrogator would say. "You're going to do the time for her crime?"

The police wouldn't let go because they knew Celeste was involved. But they needed Tracey's testimony.

"The first mistake Celeste made was that she wasn't in the same bed as Steven," Orange said. "When medics arrived, she came into the room and was clearly not sleeping with her husband. Surely that would raise a few eyebrows with police."

"They kept pressuring Tracey," Fanning said. "Trying to get her to give up Celeste because they knew there was no reason for Tracey to do this completely on her own."

Tracey would remain silent. She would wait in her jail cell for the visit from the love of her life, Celeste Beard.

But Celeste was not going anywhere near Tracey's cell.

She now had Steven's money. She didn't need anything else.

CHAPTER EIGHT

Celeste would eventually contact Tracey again. She would go into her drama queen act again, only this time the play acting would force Tracey's hand to break up with her.

Celeste then believed she had gotten away with everything scott free. Her lesbian lover had taken the fall for the murder. She now had carte blanche to Steven's estate, selling off one of the properties for a cool two million.

But like a curse that followed her around throughout her life, all of Celeste's ill-gotten gains would be short lived.

Celeste would marry Cole Johnson, a local bartender, and part-time musician she would meet in a bar in Aspen, Colorado.

Problem was that Tracey would find out about the union.

"Tracey became enraged when she read the marriage announcement," Orange said. "Here she was taking the fall for someone that she believed had loved her. Now this woman was off to a honeymoon in Aspen, Colorado. At that point, she had to realize that Steven was the victim and not her. She must have felt a sinking in her stomach at the realization that she was being played for so long."

Tracey informed the warden that she was ready to talk. She would tell the police the full story of what happened that night in Austin.

CHAPTER NINE

Nearly a year after orchestrating her husband's murder, Celeste Beard would be brought to trial and found guilty of first-degree murder.

"It was wonderful," Steven's daughter, Becky Beard said after Celeste's guilty verdict was announced. "It was absolutely wonderful. It was 'thank you, Lord.'"

"What brought Celeste down was greed," Fanning said. "Self-centeredness. And a willingness to do anything she wanted no matter who stood in the way."

"celeste had initially arrived at Steven's estate with one box of all of her possessions," Orange said. "Steven, in turn, gave her a lake house, a mansion, diamond jewelry, and allowed her to no longer have to work for a living. And how did she repay him? She killed his ass."

Steven Beard's family was allowed to address Celeste during sentencing. His son, Steven, told Celeste to go burn in hell.

But Celeste's own daughter turned on her.

"You say we turned on you," Kristina said. "Well, you turned on us. You turned on the whole Beard family. He let you into his home, loved you, honored, obeyed you, and you violated him and murdered him...Shame on you!"

Celeste will not be eligible for parole until the age of 80. She did not receive the six million "owed" to her after Steven's death. The proceeds of the Beard estate went toward his own children but also to Celeste's daughters, whom he had adopted.

Celeste continues to deny her involvement and now blames her incarceration on her daughters.

"They had two million reasons to lie," she said from her jail cell.

SHE MATES, SHE KILLS: THE TRUE STORY OF TAUSHA MORTON

ALISON YALE

AN AGGRESSIVE FLIRT

Dewayne Barrentine met Tausha Morton in early 2007.

She worked as a teacher's assistant at his son's daycare. A single parent, Barrentine would pick up his son and would be greeted by Tausha on a daily basis.

"Whenever I would pick him up," Barrentine said. "She would always make sure to step out into the hallway and give him a hug and say 'hey' to me. She made herself very noticeable."

Tausha gave Barrentine all of the hints that she was interested. The sideways glance, the smile that lingered just a little too long. But still, he needed extra coaxing.

"One of her co-workers actually approached me," Barrentine recalled when a woman in the hallway had passed him a note.

"She said, 'It's a phone number,' I said, 'To who?' She said 'Miss Tausha and she wants you go give her a call tonight. And it started from there."

Smitten by the forward nature of the sweet-faced single mother, Barrentine fell hard.

The two began dating and began living together within a month.

"She was really there for my son...," Barrentine recalled. "I had full custody of him. He would lay in the bed next to me ... and I would hear him say his prayers and he would pray for a mama." He would soon feel the same way about Tausha's daughter, Lexie.

"We weren't dating even a month and she said, 'Will you be my daddy?' And I said, 'Baby, I'll be whatever you want me to be...'"

From that moment, Barrentine became hooked as Tausha made him feel as if she really loved him. She did all the little things from kind words to love letters.

He soon began to realize, however, that Tausha had a manipulative, lying nature.

The tall tales began to pile up. She told Barrentine that she had a "Bachelor's degree in Criminal Justice" as well as an inheritance due to her from an inhertiance.

"It was from her granddad who was a federal judge who was blinded by a battery blowing up in his face. If he was a federal judge, surely his name would be on docs under Google somewhere, but I never found anything."

Barrentine grew increasingly suspicious with Tausha's stories. He did some online investigating and discovered that she had a previous marriage with a man named Mitch Kemp. He confronted her about it and she would state that she had been married five times before.

The two vaguely resembled each other, big Southern boys, "teddy bears" that were more than a little overweight.

After eight months of co-habitation, Barrentine caught Tausha cheating on him.

He promptly threw her out of his home.

"I called the Sheriff's department," Barrentine recalled. "I was like, 'look, I don't care what y'all do with her, she's got to get her shit and get outta my house.'"

Wanting retribution of some sort, Barrentine accessed Tausha's MySpace account as he knew her password.

"Dewayne gets on her Myspace account basically to mess with her," prosecutor Richard Hicks said.

After sifting through her e-mails, Barrentine would make a shocking discovery.

"I found two or three e-mails," Barrentine said. "And they were from Mitch Kemp's sister-in-law."

Mischele Kemp had written Tausha an e-mail with the subject "We're really concerned."

"How is Mitch doing? We haven't heard from you in over our year? We would like to hear from you. If we don't hear from you immediately we will contact law enforcement and media. It is not like Mitch to disappear for years on end without contacting his mother and we have became extremely concerned. Please contact us. We are very worried about him and your entire family. Sincerely, MK."

Digging a little deeper, Barrentine looked into Tausha's "sent message" box and it did not appear that she had ever responded.

"Immediately, I changed the password on the account," Barrentine said. "To where she couldn't access it and I printed off all those e-mails."

His actions would prove to be something bigger than a missing persons case. He would bring all of this information to the local police chief in Florida who instructed him to keep things to himself as he sorted things out with the Boone County Sheriff's Department in Missouri.

WHO WAS TAUSHA MORTON?

Tausha Morton, AKA Tausha Fields, met Mitch Kemp in 2001 when she lived in Colombia, Missouri.

Mitch worked as a carpet installer and had been recently divorced after fourteen years of marriage.

"It wasn't long after he got divorced that he met Tausha," Mitch's brother Rick said. "I would say within months."

Despite their eleven year age difference, Kemp fell hard for the young and vivacious Tausha.

Tausha was the proverbial "people person." Most of her friends and neighbors described her as someone who would make you welcome and treat you as if you were a long lost friend.

"She was bubbly," said one of Tausha's former employers. "Friendly and inquisitive. She paid attention and asked lots of questions about you."

Tausha liked learning about other people. She, in turn, would be all too willing to share details of her own struggles.

"She told us how her whole family was killed in a car accident," Rick Kemp said.

Tausha had a way of getting people to feel sorry for her. She would come across as a heavily burdened individual who suffered a lot of tragedy. People listening to her story would feel compassion for her lot in life and do what they could to help her.

Mitch Kemp listened intently to Tausha's tales of woe, buying them hook, line and sinker. He wanted to help her. To be her rescuer, her knight in shining armor.

The two began to date and by September of 2002, Tausha gave birth to a baby girl.

Mitch loved kids and was ecstatic. He proposed marriage and Tausha accepted.

"They got married in Pensacola," Rick said. "It was a very easy wedding."

The marriage seemed to look okay from all observers. Mitch's family didn't have any misgivings about Tausha, her charm enabling her to get into their good graces, at least at first.

"She was a really sweet girl," Carcle Kemp said, recalling her first meeting with Tausha.

But over time, his family began to notice a personality change in Mitch. Sister Mischelle stated that he wasn't "as playful as he used to be."

Family gatherings would "take a back seat to things that she wanted to do" according to Tracy Kemp, who blamed Tausha's ability to manipulate.

As work responsibilities increased for Mitch, things began to go south in their marriage very fast.

DOMESTIC LIFE AIN'T FOR ME

Bored that she was left alone with the baby, the high-strung Tausha needed an outlet.

She would arrive at her friend's gym, the Body Zone, with her baby in tow. Soon she began working part time at the fitness center.

It was there that she would meet Greg Morton.

Morton was more physically fit than Kemp but he fit the same profile psychologically. He had recently broken up with a longtime girlfriend and was be vulnerable to the manipulative charms of Tausha.

"Greg was despondent over his break-up," a family friend said. "But when he met Tausha, he kinda perked back up."

Tausha used the same seductive strategy on Morton as she used on Kemp. She detailed her tragic back story. She told him stories of being molested, of being raped.

She also told Morton in no uncertain terms that her marriage with Kemp was on the outs. Making herself look like the victim, she told Morton that Kemp had made her miserable. He was abusive, bothered her constantly and threatened physical harm.

"She told him a bunch of lies," one of Tausha's friends said. "She said she was getting him (Mitch) served, that they were getting divorced."

By February 2004, her allegations of physical abuse would be reported to the police department as Tausha filed assault charges against him.

"She said he abused her," Rick Kemp said. "By assaulting her, or slapping her or something."

Tausha informed police that she and Mitch had gotten into an argument. Then he hauled off and hit her.

Mitch Kemp would plead guilty to the charges and spend over a month in jail. Upon his release, he would be in for another surprise.

Tausha had moved out of the family home and moved in with Greg Morton, taking Lexie with her. Morton had own a farm outside of Colombia, Missouri, a sizable estate that he inherited from his step-father.

A custody battle then ensued between Tausha and Mitch for their daughter. The fight would get uglier by the day with daily phone calls between the two and their attorneys. She would refuse to allow Mitch to see Lexie and used the courts to prevent visitation.

But Mitch Kemp would not give up without a fight.

"If he had to go through the court system to do it, he would do it," Mitch's brother Rick said. "But that he was going to see his daughter."

Tausha would state that their divorce was finalized in August as the custody battle lingered on. She would then marry Greg Morton the same month.

But Morton had no idea what he was getting into and a "triangle" domestic dispute ensued.

Tausha had arranged to meet with Mitch in order to get some personal belongings. She drove in with Greg to the house of Mitch's friend where he was staying. Mitch confronted Tausha on the front porch where he immediately berated her, screaming insults.

Greg was waiting in the car at the time and went to intervene on Tausha's behalf. Mitch became further enraged and hit Greg over the head with a patio chair.

Retreating, Greg and Tausha sprinted back to the car.

Mitch, however, would disappear after that confrontation.

THE DISAPPEARANCE OF MITCH KEMP

It took awhile for Mitch's disappearance to hit home for his family members and friends. He was the type of man whom you would not hear from from awhile but would suddenly show up on the front porch.

He was dutiful about calling his mother Carole and when she didn't hear from him, she began to worry.

"We called the Boone County Sheriff's office," Rick Kemp said. "About two weeks afterward, probably. We told them that Mitch had disappeared."

The Sheriff's department did not think any foul play was involved. They offered assurance to the family that Mitch "probably didn't want to be found."

Boone County detectives came to that conclusion after they found out that Mitch was wanted for stealing some goods from a friend. They believed he disappeared in order to escape from repercussions of his actions.

Meanwhile, Greg and Tausha were living large. In late 2004, Greg put up his farm for sale which surprised both his friends and family. He treasured the land as it was bequeathed to him from his stepfather. Those close to him believed that Tausha had put him up to it.

In February of 2005, the sale of the farm finalized. With a $275,000 payout in hand, he and Tausha left Missouri, telling no one.

The Kemp family continued to believe that Mitch was not missing and that Tausha was involved somehow. They just didn't have any evidence or clues. Just a damn strong suspicion.

"Something had either happened to Mitch that had nothing to do with Tausha," Rick Kemp said. "Or something happened to Mitch and Tausha had something to do with it."

Both the Kemp family and Boone County law enforcement would then find locating Tausha and Greg to be a fruitless exercise. They literally disappeared from the face of the earth, wanting a new life. Leaving no trail behind, Tausha and Greg would move all the way to the Gulf Coast.

Greg, still smitten by Tausha, would get a tattoo of her name on his back as if he were a branded cow. With a new man firmly under her control, Tausha would go on a spending spree which included getting breast implants with Greg's money.

NO SIGN OF MITCH

By February of 2008, the Kemp family still had not heard from Mitch.

"They took a missing persons report," Rick Kemp said. "But the case went cold, quite frankly, because they didn't do anything about it."

But the Kemp family would not give up hope. They continued their search, turning to the Internet to look for any trace of their beloved son and brother.

They would search different social networking sites and court systems to look for any trace of Mitch.

They found nothing for years.

Until Mischelle Kemp found Tausha on MySpace, the social networking account.

"My sister-in-law found an account," Rick Kemp said. "That had Tausha's name and picture on it."

Mischelle immediately sent Tausha an e-mail.

"Tausha didn't respond," Rick Kemp said. "But Dewayne Berrentine did."

REVENGE SEEKING BOYFRIEND TO THE RESCUE

Dewayne Berrentine read through Tausha's e-mails on MySpace and began connecting the dots.

"Her little stories," Berrentine said. "Just because somebody lies to me, that doesn't mean I'm going to call you out on it immediately. I thought that she was coming up with these stories to impress me, maybe?"

Dewayne had discovered that Tausha had gotten around. He received some disturbing information from a man that Tausha had dated after she met Greg and before she met Dewayne.

His name was Keith Jones.

"I was in love with her and anything else didn't matter," Jones recalled. "You couldn't verify anything that she said," he says. "You know, and I mean there were a lot of stories."

Keith and Dewayne exchanged notes and stories about Tausha. They realized that she told them the same outlandish stories. But then Jones told Dewayne a story that he didn't hear before.

He described how Tausha revealed to him that she was involved in the murder of one of her exes.

"She had a few drinks in her," Jones recalled. "She said this guy had raped her and her daughter. And she apparently ... went to where he was and lured him back to her house ... and he walked in the front door. And that's when Greg shot him in the chest."

Both men thought the story was "so far-fetched" and because of the lies they always heard from her, thought nothing of it.

Dewayne did eventually confront Tausha about the allegation and she dismissed it out of hand, saying that her ex-boyfriend would say anything to throw a wrench into her new relationship.

Dewayne would change his mind about things when he opened Mischelle Kemp's e-mail message to Tausha, however. After notifying the authorities, he also wrote Mischelle Kemp back who in turn contacted the authorities in Boone County. The Sheriff's department then reopened the case. After doing some sniffing around, they discovered that Mitch had "fallen off the face of the earth" and had not filed taxes in over four years.

Finally, the Boone County Sheriff department realized that something was wrong.

INVESTIGATING TAUSHA

Detectives decided to start researching the background of Tausha.

They would discover that Tausha's parents were alive contrary to her account that they were both dead. Mitch's mother had spoken to Tausha's father shortly before her soon was to be married.

"She said, 'Mitch, we need to talk,'" recalled Rick Kemp. "You've heard a bunch of stories. Her family wasn't killed in a car wreck. They're alive. They don't want anything to do with Tausha. They say she's nothing but trouble."

Mitch dismissed the notion of his mother. He was totally smitten with Tausha.

Further investigations would reveal that Tausha had been married and divorced twice by the time she met Mitch Kemp. She would go onto have four marriages before she was thirty and the number of men she lived were numerous. Mitch had no idea that Tausha went from one man to the next man to the next. Even if he did, he was so smitten by her early in their relationship that he would have probably ignored the red flags.

Investigators would further discover that her divorce to Kemp was never finalized so she may have married Greg Morton while she was still married to Kemp.

Tracking her movements after she moved from Missouri proved difficult. Tausha and Greg were eventually tracked to Alabama.

The couple lived an indulgent lifestyle, buying luxury homes and cars on the $275,000 sale they profited after selling the farm.

But it didn't take long for them to blow through the money.

Needing more income to support Tausha, Greg would go to Mississippi in the hopes of finding clean-up work after Hurricane Katrina hit. After he left, Tausha saw it as an opportunity to cut him loose.

She had to find someone new.

"While he was gone doing Katrina," Barrentine said. "She was blowing through his money. Then he came home finding another man laying in his bed and he's broke."

Greg would immediately file for divorce.

MEN AND MORE MEN

Cut off from her money supply from Greg, Tausha would find work as an assistant at a day care center. It was there that she would meet Dewayne Barrentine.

She would follow the same modus operandi in her seduction of Barrentine, telling him the sob stories of her life. She described how Greg Morton would abuse her and how she escaped. She gave details on how Greg would try to "jump on her" and that they had "several physical altercations."

Agreeing to let her move in, Dewayne would meet Greg when he was helping Tausha get her belongings out of his house.

The two didn't fight. Instead, they spoke briefly and Greg would later tell Dewayne about how detectives from Missouri were looking to speak with Tausha.

Barrentine would eventually discover Tausha cheating on him and throw her out of his home. She would find a new boyfriend a few days later by the name of Denver Workman.

Workman left his job and his extended family from Florida to Wilmington, Delaware after Tausha begged him to do so. Then she wanted him to move back and Workman refused.

"She would yell, scream and throw things at me because I wasn't leaving," Workman recalled. "She would tell Lexie I was a bad person and to kick me. I bought her a bus ticket to Florida and let her borrow my truck that was still down there. She took the truck, and I never saw her again."

Police would finally catch up to Tausha in Dothan, Alabama and confront her about the disappearance of Mitch Kemp.

During her initial interrogation, Tausha would firmly deny having any contact with Mitch.

"What do you mean what happened to Mitch?" Tausha would ask detectives in bewilderment. "I haven't had any contact with him. None."

The investigators continued to press, however, and Tausha would try to insinuate Greg as having something to do with Mitch's disappearance.

"They had words on the phone," Tausha told detectives. "And then they had, they got in a fist fight one time."

After being threatened with the possibility of being put in jail and leaving her five year old daughter Lexie in the hands of the state, Tausha then placed the blame on Greg.

"Greg killed Mitch," Tausha said. "He told me."

She would then inform detectives that she wasn't there when it happened. She stated that Greg left about 45 minutes later after he had yet another phone conversation with Mitch.

Tausha would claim that she feared for both her and her child's life because of Greg's temper.

She would recall that Greg shot Mitch on the farm. Investigators played along, even paying for her plane ticket to fly from Alabama to Missouri in order to let them know where Greg had buried Mitch. But once she arrived, Tausha seemed confused by the layout of the farm. She could not pinpoint where exactly the body had been buried.

She was then released under her own recognizance back to Alabama while Sheriff deputies proceeded to dig up the farm to no avail. They used ground penetrating radar, cadaver sniffing dogs but came up empty.

WHERE WAS GREG MORTON?

While talks with Tausha revealed some clues, investigators were even more eager to speak with Greg Morton.

After ending his marriage with Tausha, he settled in St. Louis. He was going to school to become an electrician and had a new girlfriend.

He wanted nothing further to do with Tausha. When investigators approached him, Greg immediately invoked his right to an attorney and refused to speak further.

Detectives did not have enough evidence to charge him. But they had Tausha on the run and spoke to her again. This go around, they decided to employ a little psychological manipulation.

"But I tell you what," Detective Dave Wilson said while sitting across from Tausha in the interrogation room. "He (Greg Morton) automatically assumed that you talked to us. Now, we didn't confirm that."

"Why did he think that?" Tausha asked.

"Well, there's only...who knows?"

"But he said he thought he'd talk to you?"

"I'm going to ask you again. Can you take us directly to where that hole was?"

This go around, Tausha said yes. The Boone County Sheriff's department flew her in from Alabama yet again to Greg Morton's farm.

This time, Tausha led investigators straight to where the body was buried.

Mitch Kemp's remains were dug up and his identity was confirmed.

"It didn't surprise us," Rick Kemp said. "But we were all just blown away. I mean, I just didn't want to believe that my brother was gone."

Investigators discovered that Mitch had been shot numerous times and found numerous shell casings in the makeshift grave. They then went to St. Louis and arrested Greg Morton.

"He wasn't surprised when we showed up," Detective Wilson recalled.

Tausha was allowed to return home but investigators had a suspicion that she was more involved than she let on.

A VOW OF SILENCE

Greg strangely refused to rat out Tausha, remaining in prison until he was officially charged.

Tausha moved to Texas, however, and began dating someone new. Investigators would catch up with her again, however, and this time a heated ninety-minute interrogation would ensue.

Their probing questions would force Tausha to change her story about Mitch's murder completely.

"I did not do anything," Tausha said after detectives informed her that she would be charged with first-degree murder. "I helped you in every way I could possibly fucking help you.

"Tausha," Detective Wilson said slowly. "We got people who say, say otherwise, okay."

Tausha then changed her story again, stating that she was present when Greg murdered Mitch.

"I snuck around behind Greg's back and I saw Mitch, okay," Tausha said. "Greg had no idea."

She stated Greg would kill Mitch in a jealous rage after they returned from a hotel for a tryst. They then drove back to the farm and Greg assaulted Mitch before he got out of the car.

"He had a gun in his hands," Tausha said. "It was a black gun. Mitch started walking backwards. I ran inside the house and then I ran back outside. I saw that Mitch was walking backwards, and Greg was walking towards him. And Greg shot him. I didn't kill Mitch. I didn't want Mitch to die."

But the investigators didn't see it that way. They charged her with first-degree murder.

THE TRIAL

In June of 2009, Tausha had been imprisoned for over six months as she awaited trial.

Her bail was set at one million dollars.

Greg Morton then decided it was time to cut a deal. He broke his silence on what really happened the day of Mitch Kemp's murder. He would admit to his involvement in exchange for a more lenient sentence if he testified against Tausha.

In 2010, Tausha's trial began.

The prosecution's argument was that Tausha was the mastermind behind the murder, that even though Greg pulled the trigger it was Tausha that put the idea in his head. They also believed that Tausha's motive was to have sole custody of their daughter.

The defense would claim that Tausha was innocent and the victim. Her attorney was, in essence, using the same technique that Tausha used on all of her men. They would play on sympathy and hope that the jury would be as charmed by Tausha as all of her men.

GREG MORTON CONFESSES

Morton would take the stand and tell the jury exactly how Tausha manipulated him to kill Mitch.

"She's hysterical," Morton recalled. "She said Mitch raped her."

"What are you feeling, Greg, at this point?" Prosecutor Hicks asked.

"I wanted retribution. Tausha took charge and handed me a gun the net morning. She goes, 'I'm going to get Mitch, and when I get back, you shoot him.'"

"What were you going to do, Greg?"

"I was going to do what she asked me to do."

"They made a plan in that Tausha was going to go in town and pick Mitch up," Rick Kemp said. "And tell him that Greg was out of town."

Mitch arrived at the farm, thinking that it would only be the two of them. But then Greg emerged from the porch.

"I had a gun in my hand," Morton recalled. "I raised it and pointed it at him. I kinda paused I was kinda struggling with it a little bit. And then she started yelling at me to shoot him."

Greg believed that he was committing a protective act. He believed that Mitch was raping Tausha and molesting their six-year-old daughter.

"Then she said 'You got to get something to move him. Get something to move him with." Greg recalled. "Then she said, 'Come on. You should have had this ready.'"

"And you saw that she was still struggling?"

"He was."

"So what did you do?"

"I shot him again."

"Was he struggling anymore?"

"It was over," Morton said. "I used farm equipment to pick up Mitch's body and we buried him in a pit. When we were rolling the dirty on Mitch she said 'Mitch Kemp is a piece of shit and nobody is going to look for him for a long time.'"

The defense would then call a neighbor who testified on Tausha's behalf, stating that she thought she was under Greg's control.

Greg then broke down on the stand and tearfully apologized to Mitch Kemp's family.

Over time, however, he began to realize that Tausha was a cunning liar. As he got to know her better, he realized that he had been duped.

"He'd been played like a fiddle by her," Rick Kemp said. "She did it to every man that she had."

Tausha was not called to the stand by the defense and the jury would find her guilty.

"I think she thought she was going to walk," Rick Kemp said. "She thought she could just get away with lying and manipulating people."

Tausha Morton was sentenced to life in prison without parole but is currently appealing her sentencing.

SHEILA LABARRE

79

RICK STACKHOUSE

The farmhouse and surrounding area looked like something from the set of "Little House on the Prairie."

The house on Harvey Farm stood nestled in between tall pine trees, peaceful streams, and wildlife.

A place where you don't expect to find scenes that would be given an "X" rating if it were a horror movie.

The police arrived at the home while conducting a search for a missing young man named Kenneth Countje. They did not have to search far to find evidence of criminal activity. In the front of the property, lay a mattress burning alongside a smoking garbage barrel.

Their first inclination was to believe that the resident was burning garbage. A citation was due, maybe, but they had more pressing matters to attend to.

But upon closer inspection of the barrel, the officers saw a bone sticking out of the garbage.

A femur?

A mass of fleshy goo remained at the knob of the bone and the smell of the charred remains made the policemen gag.

They both gave each other a look of horror. Here in a town where the most serious crime would be a speeding ticket or jaywalking, the police were about to enter a whole world of horror beyond their wildest imagination.

CHAPTER ONE

Epping, New Hampshire.

Population = less than six thousand.

Epping is a rainy, small town that has been sarcastically nicknamed "The Center of the Universe". That has not stopped the residents from hosting parades, canoe races and music festivals. But when Sheila LaBarre arrived, the tiny hamlet soon became known for murder.

"She was a smart woman," forensic psychologist Paula Orange said. "Not book smart but intuitive. She could read people."

Sheila was born Sheila Kaye Bailey in Fort Payne, Alabama in 1958.

She was the youngest of six children. Her first marriage with a man named Ronnie Jennings would last less than two months. Jennings would find out that Sheila had been locking his child from a previous marriage in a closet to punish her. Jennings would divorce Sheila but she would find herself a new man in short order, tying the knot with John Baxter and moving to Chattanooga, Tennessee. Even though married, she would secretly fantasize about being swept away by a rich man. Sheila's mental illness would come to bear in her second marriage and that would end in divorce as well. Despondent, Sheila tried to kill herself and was sent to a psychiatric facility. She would be raped by an orderly inside the hospital.

Now single in Tennessee, the cash-strapped Sheila was forced to live in a local YMCA. She attended a church service and had a private talk with one of the preachers as she wanted "spiritual guidance." She would later claim that the reverend asked if she wanted to "sit in his lap." She then went to a psychiatrist who asked her if she had anal sex with any of her former husbands. The doctor then called Sheila at home and asked if "what she was wearing" and if she "was touching herself."

"If what we are to believe all of Sheila's stories," Orange said. "Then literally all of her interactions with men have ended with them as the pervert and her as the victim. Her sister would later testify that Sheila was molested by her father when she was young. Then her abusive marriages, the rape at the psych facility segues into a spiritual search where she meets a preacher who shows her the tent in his pants. Crazy."

CHAPTER TWO

Sheila turned to personal ads after her failures in marriage. She didn't like the normal courtship process of going to bars and meeting men there. She used the personal ads to cherry pick the men she wanted, men she could dominate.

"Whether on-line or off-line, Sheila behaved like a woman who was in complete control," Orange said. "She would develop a strange kind of power over men. It was almost as if she knew which men would be vulnerable to her feminine wiles and which ones would fight back. But when it came to Dr. Bill LaBarre, it was more of a case of getting the money."

While in Tennessee, Dr. LaBarre decided to take out a personal ad. He would get a response from Sheila who immediately sought to separate herself from the other paramours of the rich doctor.

She sent the doctor nude Polaroids of herself.

The strategy worked.

"She showed no shame in flirting with the older man and soon had him in the palm of her hand," Orange said. "He'd buy her fancy clothes, necklaces, the whole nine yards."

Wilfred "Bill" LaBarre was a successful chiropractor but lonely. Overweight and bespectacled, he had little to offer aside from his wealth. He was in his sixties and recently widowed.

Dr. Labarre was considered a good man by all who knew him. He had been the "Chiropractor of the Year" in 1983 but that would be the same year his beloved Edwina would pass away from cancer. Eager to salve the loneliness, he married another woman named Leona but she abandoned the doctor after a few years. He had two children from his first marriage; Laura and Gregory.

Now alone and widowed, the doctor wanted to spend his golden years enjoying his wealth.

And a young woman.

He would look at the nude Polaroids of the curvaceous Southern Belle, becoming obsessed.

"Here was a lonely, older man who all of a sudden had a 27-year old woman sending him nude photos. He thought he hit the jackpot."

Dr. LaBarre soon invited Sheila to come live with him at his farm in Epping, New Hampshire. The farm was a spacious one, a 115-acre horse ranch that according to LaBarre, "needed a female hand."

Sheila would become enamored by life on the farm, at least at first. She "never heard a June bug before" and the isolated country home gave her a peace that she never experienced.

Neighbors were not shocked that Dr. LaBarre took in such a younger woman as his girlfriend. He reportedly had other girlfriends after his wife died. "Sheila ran all the other girls off," one neighbor said.

But Sheila would prove to be a high-maintenance girlfriend. She would drain Dr. LaBarre's finances, making him buy her gifts and prizes which included a brand-new Silver Mercedes.

She also began to interject herself into LaBarre's estate and business dealings.

The farm that LaBarre owned was called the Old Harvey Farm. It was named after the original owners of the property who still lived in the area. But Sheila forced the doctor to change the name, she wanted it called something that reflected her personality.

The Silver Leopard Farm.

Sheila then had a sign made up and had it placed at the entrance.

She was marking her territory.

CHAPTER THREE

Despite the constant gifts and financial prizes, Sylvia proved to be an ungrateful sugar baby. The relationship would turn tempestuous after a few months. Sheila would claim that Dr. LaBarre often referred to himself as an "old fart" and looked the other way when Sheila began to have different men over for sex.

"He just worried about me when I would date far from home. But he was getting old and his heart would stop beating sometimes."

But the couple fought and police were routinely called to the residence to mediate their domestic disputes.

"You would sometimes hear gunshots," Bruce Allen, a LaBarre neighbor said. "You would hear her screaming, 'I'm going to kill you, you mother fucker!'"

Sheila once pulled a gun on the doctor and forced him out of the home. The chiropractor hid behind a boulder as his girlfriend shot at him.

LaBarre's daughter also recalled that she heard Sheila screaming threats at her father. "I'm gonna kill the horses and I'm going to kill you too."

Laura would later remark at how much her father changed after Sheila came into his life. He went from a normal, well-liked member of the community to a meek, submissive man.

"Sheila was all about being an opportunist," Orange said. "She had the ability to read a man, analyzing his weaknesses, size him up and then push the buttons. With LaBarre, she had a lonely man in front of her. He would tolerate anything in order not to lose her at first and then he simply became fearful of his life. These men in this small New England town did not have the wherewithal to deal with a violent sociopath like Sheila."

Sheila didn't stop with the renaming of Old Harvey Home. She soon took over the accounting duties at LaBarre's chiropractic business. She began organizing the practice into a well-oiled machine. She would track down patients who owed the doctor money and file numerous small claims in the Hampton District Court.

Concerned friends would advise him to dump Sheila before it was too late but it became apparent that the doctor either didn't know how or was afraid to. Dr. LaBarre informed neighbor Bruce Allen that he "had to get rid of her" and that he wanted to "send her back to Alabama. Hopefully, she'll stay there."

Her power over Dr. LaBarre increased to the point where he had given her power of attorney. She began rewriting his will, becoming the executor of his estate. The will stated that he was leaving everything to "a very special lady known as Sheila Kaye Jennings LaBarre."

"The will was very carefully redacted from the original," Orange said. "She kept a lot of the parts of the original and used her own typewriter to amend the little detail of where all the assets will go to. She was very astute and covered her tracks very well for someone who was supposedly schizophrenic."

The two would live together (Sheila would move out briefly but claim to be his common-law wife) from 1987 until LaBarre's death in 2000 at the age of 74. The coroner logged his cause of death as heart disease. There were suspicions among those close to the doctor that believe Sheila poisoned him to hasten the process.

"He was pretty old," Orange said. "And according to the autopsy, the heart disease was significant. So Sheila didn't have anything to do with his death despite the suspicions. The killings would come later."

Sheila would inherit the farm, LaBarre's Chiropractor office, two apartments and a rental home.

This was all valued at over two million dollars in assets.

Strangely, Sheila would marry a Jamaican national named Wayne Ennis in August of 1995 while living with Dr. LaBarre. Ennis drove a tour bus around Jamaica and Sheila made sure that when she toured the islands with Dr. LaBarre that they would cross paths with her Jamaican lover. She arranged for Ennis to obtain a visa and took him back to the farm with her. She would later claim that she and the doctor had stopped having sex and that she "had needs" which apparently Ennis took care of. She would later concede to pleasing the doctor sexually, "I'd use my hand," she said afterward.

Ennis would live in the farmhouse for almost a year. He had his own numerous encounters with Sheila which were violent and bizarre. One night, she ordered him to get in the car. The two then drove around the quiet town, Sheila's voice taking on a conspiratorial tone.

"I wish one of those damn horses would just kick him (Dr. LaBarre) in the head," Sheila said. "Kick him in the head and kill his old ass. I've thought about strangling him myself. But now I have a better idea. I want you to kill him."

Ennis was too frightened to say no to Sheila. The two would eventually divorce and the court records reveal that Sheila took out a restraining order against him.

Ennis disputed the allegations and stated that Sheila was the abuser.

He would later recall being punched, pushed, and shot at by Sheila.

"She told me that she was going to send me back to Jamaica in a box," Ennis said.

Dr. LaBarre told Ennis that Sheila was crazy and believed that she would eventually kill him. He gave the Jamaican money and sent him to the bus station, requesting that he leave town for his own safety.

After the relationship with Ennis ended, Sheila began dating James Brackett.

She and James would remain together for six years despite the fact that Sheila would attack Brackett with a pair of scissors, a machete, and an ax. When all of that failed she tried to shoot him.

The two would break up after which Brackett would get himself a vanity license plate that read "I'm Alive."

Brackett recalled moments where Sheila would act sweet and nice only to go into a violent rage moments later. He said that the greatest example was a time when he was taking a long bath with Sheila only to have her get out of the tub and smash him in the face with a two-foot grill brush.

Two of his teeth would be knocked out from the impact.

Sheila would attack Brackett for a variety of transgressions that would not be guilty of. Hurting her rabbits, damaging her property or having affairs with other women.

Brackett finally had enough, escaping from the farm on one rainy night and hitchhiking back into town.

"I'm lucky to be alive," he would later state.

CHAPTER FOUR

Sheila inherited the farm after LaBarre's death. The doctor's children tried to contest the will but were told that the odds of winning the case were 50/50 at best. They would also have to front over $50,000 to pay for the court costs.

Sheila soon turned the farm into her own private fiefdom. She would hire young men to help her around the place then pay them with her sexual favors or sometimes just beat the shit out of them.

"There would neighbors that would claim to see young men leave her house," Orange said. "They would look beaten up; black eyes, bloody lips, facial contusions. God knows what else."

Her neighbors began to suspect something fishy was going on but had no real evidence to call the police with.

"The first time I met Sheila LaBarre was at the Harvey Farm Stand," said Bonnie Meroth, one of Sheila's neighbors. "It was during the summertime when the produce was ready. I had no basic interaction with her except that of someone standing next to another person as a consumer. And she suddenly turned around and said 'I'll kill you if you come down to my farm' or words to that effect."

Bonnie would later claim that Sheila would try to scare her while driving down the road, nearly running her over while she was on her morning walk.

When she wasn't intimidating neighbors and townsfolk, Sheila would use the farm as the playground for her own private fetishes.

She liked to control and bully men. Stroking one of her pet rabbits, she would punish and insult the men unlucky enough to work at her farm.

"Are you kidding me?" Sheila yelled at the young man who dropped the wheelbarrow. "This should have been done yesterday."

He was young and naive, needing money. If it meant taking lip from Sheila, so be it. He needed work and she seemed nice when she hired him.

"Hurry up!" Sheila said, kicking the man in his buttocks. "Move, move. Are you kidding me? I've never seen a lazier man in my life."

Fatigued after working sixteen hours for seven days straight, the young man keeled over in exhaustion, dropping the wheelbarrow.

"Bitch made, perverted ass pedophile!" Sheila said. "Is this what I am paying you for? I am paying you to work. Now get off your bitch ass. Now!"

It became apparent that Sheila had a gift. A gift of controlling a certain type of man. Verbally abusive and overbearing, she encountered very little resistance.

She kicked the young man again. "Your name is 'bitch', you hear me?"

His real name was Michael Deloge.

CHAPTER FIVE

Deloge had problems as a teen. He got caught up in drugs and found himself on the streets, living out of homeless shelters. In 2004, he would meet Sheila LaBarre.

Deloge became smitten with the woman whom he saw as the life of the party. She would drink beer and play country songs on a guitar. According to Deloge's stepfather, Gordon Boston, the duo would indulge in drugs and study "sadistic material".

Deloge would join Sheila at her farm and soon become her personal whipping boy. Sheila would slap him around like a rag doll. One of the fellow ranch hands, Philip Sullos, recalled witnessing Sheila beating on Deloge with a hardwood stick until he bled. Deloge cowered and took the beating. She would then throw Deloge into a windowless shack and slam the door shut.

Deloge would cower meekly in the corner until Sheila came and got him, making no attempt to escape.

He would be declared missing in 2004 and no one would ever see him again.

In February of 2006, Sheila began looking for a new farmhand. She had her own criteria. He had to be young but pliable to her controlling methods.

She would find the perfect foil in Kenny Countie.

"Kenny was a lovely boy," Carolynn Lodge, Kenny's mother said. "He couldn't do enough for you. Everyone was his friend. I was so proud of him. He never had a horrible word for anybody and that was the problem. He trusted everybody."

Kenny's trust would lead him into Sheila LaBarre's trap.

Kenny would answer one of Sheila's personal ads. The young man was still naive and according to some reports had a "low IQ". The two met through a telephone personal ad service with Sheila calling up the young man and charming him in a way that no woman ever did.

"He (Kenny) told my son Brian that he met a 47-year old woman in New Hampshire," Lodge said. "She owned a farm. She owned a beautiful car. And she was rich. And he was serious about her."

"Kenny fit Sheila's psychological criteria," Orange said. "She targeted men whom she could overpower not only physically but also mentally. She was older than Kenny and light years more cunning. She knows exactly what to say and do to push his buttons. She takes the lead, telling him that he is going to be 'in for the time of his life' and that she 'can't wait to see him.' To a young man with limited experience and intelligence like Kenny, this is music to his ears."

Sheila would arrive at Kenny's home in the silver Mercedes. The silver leopard, the cougar, picking up her prey and taking him back to her lair.

Kenny's family would never see him again.

Sheila would use the same methods on Kenny as she did on the men in the past. She seduced the young man first then isolated him in her farmhouse. Then she berated him verbally before beating the shit out of him with face slaps, punches, and a wooden stick.

The beatings would come to a head during a weekend in February of 2000. Sheila beat Kenny's face into a pulp, took the wooden cane to his legs and may have poisoned him.

Then she decided to take him shopping at Walmart.

Placing him in a wheelchair, she rolled him around the outlet as she stocked up on garden supplies. She dumped two containers of diesel fuel into the prone Kenny's lap.

Little did he know that she would later use the gas to incinerate his body.

Customers gawked at the odd couple, concerned about the contusions on Kenny's face.

"Fuck you looking at?" Sheila would scream as she sped down through the aisle.

Employees of the store soon became concerned, calling the police.

The cops would arrive, confronting the couple in the store. They inquired about Kenny's condition but he didn't respond. Instead, Sheila took the lead, telling Kenny that he "didn't have to talk to these assholes."

The police didn't follow through. Kenny remained silent as Sheila rolled him through the store and out the door. No crime had been witnessed and they let the couple go.

Kenny's mother would later sue the police for negligence but it was tossed out of court in 2010.

A few nights after the Walmart incident, Sheila would make a frantic phone call to the police.

"I got a pervert in my house!" she screamed into the phone. "He's a pedophile! A pedophile!"

In a bizarre sequence of events, Sheila began to play a recording for the detective on the other end. She had routinely audio recorded everything she did, trying to incriminate the young men she worked with into admitting they were pedophiles. On this occasion, she played back a recording of her and Kenny.

"On the tape was my son, vomiting," Lodge said. "He kept saying 'he's faking, he's faking.'"

Sheila would ask Kenny if he was a pedophile on the tape. Kenny would answer 'yes'.

"Now he's a pedophile," Kenny's mother said. "Now he's raping children. Raping his brother. He's vomiting."

The police would write off the call as the rantings of a schizophrenic. They did not immediately respond to the residence.

Sheila would then kill Kenny Countie.

"She had to justify the killing of the young men in her own mind," Orange said. "For some bizarre reason, she would brainwash herself into thinking that her victims were pedophiles. She would repeat the question like a mantra, 'Are you a pedophile? Are you a pedophile?' Working herself up into an angry and violent state of mind before she killed the man."

Sheila's sister, Lynn Noojin, believed that Sheila was sexually abused by her father. Because of this, she became obsessed with child molestation. She would accuse the young men that worked for her of various sexual deviations, including pedophilia, incest, and bestiality.

CHAPTER SIX

After the bizarre call to police, authorities would not arrive at the farmhouse until the next morning. The police would enter the grounds, seeing both the burning mattress and barrel with Kenny's remains. They would not identify the burning bones as belonging to Kenny until much later.

Sheila had murdered Kenny the night before. She attacked Kenny ferociously with a kitchen knife, pushing the already weakened young man to the floor and stabbing away.

Blood sprayed and splattered everywhere.

Sheila then dragged Kenny's body out to her yard where she doused his body with the diesel fuel they had purchased at Walmart.

Lighting a match, she set the dead man on fire. She then took her pet rabbit in her lap, pulled up a chair and watched Kenny Countie burn.

"He was dismembered," Kenny's mother said, fighting tears. "And he was put in a pit and burned. But my son, he just wanted to be loved. I can't imagine what he must have been thinking. Because he was all alone."

Police would look throughout the house and find blood splatter on the walls and floor. A forensic team arrived and matched the blood with Kenny's DNA sample from his Army days. They would find the wallet of Michael Deloge but not his body.

Hundreds of police would spend seventeen days searching the 115-acre property. They found numerous burn pits and blood remains that were so old they had layers of dust on them. They would find clothing that belonged to Deloge and some toes that remain unidentified (it is rumored that the toes may belong to a mysterious Irish man who Sheila claims was stalking her.)

Going on the run from the cops, Sheila hitchhiked along Interstate 293. She was then picked up by Stephen Martello.

"Thanks so much for stopping," Sheila said.

"No problem," Martello said, looking the buxom Southern Belle up and down. His heart began to race.

Will he get lucky?

"My car broke down about two miles back. I got into a fight with my boyfriend and I'm trying to get to Dorchester."

"I'm headed that way," Martello said.

Sheila clutched her purse as if it were a security blanket and she kept looking back at the rear window.

"You all right?" he asked.

"Yeah," Sheila said "Just a little rattled. You know, it has been a tough day."

Martello took Sheila to the drug store when she said she needed to stop off and "buy some things". He tailed Sheila around the store until she bought a douche. Noting her erratic behavior, Martello disappeared out of Sheila's earshot to call the police on his cell phone.

"Hi," Martello said. "Just curious if you folks are looking for someone who just robbed a bank or an escaped mental patient. I just met a woman who is acting kind of strange."

When the authorities informed him that they were not actively investigating someone with that kind of background, Martello took Sheila to a hotel room.

The two would engage in wild and loud sex.

"You just had sex with an angel," Sheila proclaimed after they were done.

"Is that right?"

"You're not like the other men," Sheila said. "My boyfriend, Jesus, I just caught him with a huge stack of child porn. He is a pedophile. So are all those damn cops. Pedophiles, all of them. I think all sex offenders must die."

Martello said nothing. Instead, he put his pants and shoes on as fast as he could as Sheila continued to go on another bizarre rant.

"Vengeance is mine saith the Lord," Sheila said, laying on the bed in post-coital repose. "I was sent back to earth as an angel. I know how to speak to God in Hebrew. Do it every night."

Martello excused himself and high-tailed it out of the hotel room. He arrived home and saw the television broadcast about Sheila. He didn't call the police, worried that he would be an accessory to her crimes. Instead, Martello drove to the station and practically sprinted to the front desk.

"I think I just met Sheila LaBarre."

"To the end, Sheila had control over just about every man put in front of her," Orange said. "Here was a guy who picks her up at the side of the road. He thinks she is crazy enough to where he calls the cops to find out if there are any missing mental patients. He knows that she has a screw loose but he has sex with her anyway. It may be a poor reflection on men for sure but his response is typical. The men that Sheila encountered, from Dr. LaBarre all the way to Stephen Martello, all had the same false narratives going on in their head. They did not see a beautiful woman as something evil. It just didn't fit their narrative. So when Sheila begins her abuse, they just can't believe it. They refuse to hit a 'woman' back. She gets them 'pussy whipped' then beats the shit out of them. Rinse and repeat."

Sheila LaBarre would later be arrested for the murders of Michael Deloge and Kenneth Countje. She would plead no guilty on the grounds of insanity.

"This is a sick, sick woman," her attorney would argue. "Deeply disturbed."

Court-appointed psychiatrists would agree, testifying that Sheila was delusional as well as schizophrenic.

The jury would visit both LaBarre's farm and the Walmart where she frequented first hand. Sheila would join them as well although she was forced to wear a stun belt.

The jury did not buy her insanity defense and found her guilty.

"The fact that she has to remain for the rest of her life behind bars," Kenny's mother said. "She got what she asked for. She'll never see the light of day. Horrible thing is that my son, he's not here with me. He was only twenty-four."

Sheila LaBarre is now serving life in prison without possibility of parole.

SHIRLEY WITHERS

95

LISA ARAGON

Shirley Withers and Peter Shellard looked to be a mismatched couple.

Shellard was a multi-millionaire dollar real estate mogul and high-end car dealer. Logic would dictate that he would date much younger women, seducing aspiring actresses and models with his wealth. But Shirley was anything but a supermodel. She was an ordinary looking bookkeeper, thirty-three-years-old, and bit on the frumpy side.

"He was a hot shot," forensic psychologist Paula Orange said. "An eccentric hotshot but still very well-to-do. He would strut around town wearing fancy suits with matching socks but wear sandals over them. Shirley, on the other hand, was very unassuming. She looked like the typical cubicle drone. A little overweight and plain looking. Nothing sexy about her."

Their relationship, however, would be one of the biggest firestorms of sex, murder, and drugs in Australian history.

BEGINNINGS

Shirley was born in New Delhi, India in 1966. She immigrated with her family to Australia when she was a child. She married young and had two sons with her first husband. By 2000, she would be divorced and immediately be on the market for a new beau.

Enter Peter Shellard.

Peter, born in 1949, touted himself as a self-made millionaire although he had a benefactor in an older, maternal figure in Vera Moore.

He didn't finish high school, dropping out to obtain his real estate agent's license at night. Once he acquired that, he began leveraging properties around the Brighton area eventually making a fortune in addition to buying a high-end car dealership.

He called his company "Peter Shellard Real Estate" and then used that money to help finance a deal where he took control over Kellow-Falkiner Motors. He juggled both real estate as well as used Rolls-Royce and Bentley parts.

Shellard's businesses continued to flourish. He purchased many companies as well as commercial and rental properties.

"He hung around some heavy hitters in his area," Orange said. "People who could buy Rolls Royces without batting an eye."

Shellard would purchase the Rosecraddock Place in North Caulfield, a regal mansion which would later sell for over $7 million upon his death. As his wealth grew, he began collecting high-end cars which included a 1923 Rolls-Royce, a 1951 Rolls-Royce Silver Dawn, and a Mercedez-Benz 450SL convertible.

AN ECCENTRIC NUT

Shellard did have mental issues, however, suffering from bipolar disorder.

"His mansion was filled with all kinds of knick-knacks," Orange said. "Stuff that seemed disconnected and junky. But he was bipolar and people with that ailment tend to have different eccentricities. His was to hoard stuff among other things."

Shellard was reported to be a recluse, sheltering himself from the outside world as he became more pwealthy. He had a barbed wire fence built high around the mansion but it served more to keep him in then keeping people out. His neighbors would rarely see him outside the compound unless he was walking his dogs. He also had ponies and kept an area for beehives. Neighbors complained about the bees and the city had the hives destroyed. Shellard would later file suit and demand that he have the remains of his dead bees returned.

Shellard would treat other homeowners as if they were peasants and would come and go on their private grounds as he pleased. One neighbor reported that Shellard came into their backyard and began sifting through their garden tools. Another complained that Shellard would park one of his Rolls-Royces in their personal garage. Shellard was informed to remove the vehicle after which he became enraged and began to tear apart the garage. He would then be sued for the action and was forced to pay almost $2000 in damages.

"Obviously, he walked around as if he had a sense of entitlement," Orange said. "Definitely a narcissistic sociopath but he could turn on the charm when he wanted. It all depended on what he wanted. When he was trying to make a sale, he could charm you. When he was doing something stupid and you called him on it, that is when he went berserk."

Town councilwoman Veronika Martens had plenty of bizarre dealings with Shellard as well. On one occasion, Shellard chopped down some cypress trees on his property and began burning the branches. Neighbors called to complain and firefighters came down to extinguish the flames.

Enraged, Shellard began attacking the firefighters and cut through the fire hoses with an ax.

Later, Shellard would be caught breaking into Caulfield Town Hall by climbing in through the roof. He would also come into the building unannounced, enter unoccupied offices and begin making phone calls.

"Shellard was an aggressive, anti-government guy," Orange said. "He went so far as to try to have his mansion designated as a religious place in order to avoid taxes. The judge got a good laugh at that one. The religion of what? Nutty behavior?"

Angered that his request was denied, he began making plans to tear down the mansion and divide up the land. But legal maneuverings blocked him from doing that as city council members had his mansion placed on the Historic Buildings Council, giving it legal protection.

A SADO-MASOCHIST

A ladies man, Shellard would marry twice. He had three daughters, Jenny, Clare and Sarah, before divorcing his second wife Elizabeth in 1994.

Shellard really did not have any bad habits that than his eccentricities as he abstained from both alcohol and smoking. He did have one fetish, however, and that was sadomasochism.

Shellard would go to clubs and participate in bondage sessions, preferring visits to the Hellfire Club in Brighton. Once there, he would "dress up in a full range of leather outfits and had belts with studs."

Shellard would go to the Hellfire Club to be whipped.

"He told me initially that his pain threshold was very low," Shellard's friend Christine Smith said. "And after a number of visits his tolerance for pain increased to the point where he really liked what was occurring. He found it very erotic."

By 2001, he was looking for a new partner and found one in Shirley Withers.

"Initially mum and I thought Shirley was a bit odd," Jenny, Shellard's eldest daughter recalled. "She would never look you in the eye. She was always very kind, though."

ENTER SHIRLEY WITHERS

Opposites attract, and Shellard soon began wooing Shirley with his luxurious lifestyle. He brought her numerous gifts, jewelry, and clothing.

"I'll bankroll all your dreams," he teased.

Shirley took him up on the offer, expressing her desire to run her own clothing boutique.

"Shellard did anything and everything for Shirley," forensic psychologist Paula Orange said. "He bought her everything she asked for evening financing her 'dream' of running a boutique store in a prestigious area of Brighton. Never mind the fact that Shirley had no business experience. Shellard believed he had money to burn."

"You can't be serious?" Shirley gushed when Peter told her he would buy her a clothing company.

"What are you going to call it?" Shellard asked, smiling.

"God," Shirley said. "God. I don't know. How about Suzette? Suzette Boutique?"

"Suzette Boutique!" Shellard laughed aloud as Shirley hugged him in appreciation.

Shellard made all the arrangements for Shirley to run the store. He had it designed and built to her specifications.

Shirley would have all of the brand name fashions in her store. She loaded the shelves with Marianna Hardwick, Charlie Brown, and Lisa Ho.

Shellard had one caveat and that was having his eldest daughter, Jenny, work in the boutique. Jenny herself, however, had a less than flattering impression of both Shirley and her attempts to run a business.

"My first impression when I started working there was that it was just a mess," Jenny said. "I couldn't understand how Shirley kept paying us every week. I had seen invoices totaling thousands of dollars and wondered where Shirley was getting the money. Shirley would just continuously buy stock for the business and for herself. She definitely had a problem with spending money."

Shellard did not stop at just buying Shirley her own boutique.

He bought her a house.

"It was a bit of an odd arrangement," Orange said. "They had separate living quarters. Shellard wanted his own house to himself and would visit Shirley for coital purposes."

Shellard displayed further bad judgment when he allowed Shirley to be put in charge of the accounting of his car dealership.

"He figured she was a bookkeeper," Orange said. "She must know what she's doing."

Shellard's naivete didn't end there as he allowed Shirley access to his property accounts in addition to becoming a signatory on his car dealership.

What Shellard didn't take into account was that Shirley was not a person he could trust nor did she know what she was doing.

Her boutique began to fail. She had purchased too much product and the few items that did sell would not have a high enough margin. Being a marginal business person, she continued to purchase inventory despite not generating any revenue.

The store began losing money. Lost of it.

So Shirley took it upon herself to begin stealing from Shellard's dealership. She would write checks to herself in upwards of $10,000. Shellard began noticing the discrepancies and called in his accountant.

After checking the books, the two realized that Shirley stole over $900,000, a significant amount of Shellard's wealth.

NO CURE FOR A SPENDAHOLIC

Shellard owned over eleven properties and his total net worth looked to be about $10-15 million.

By the time Shellard had finally got wind of Shirley's financial doings, she had amassed over $43,000 in credit card debt while her store was almost $275,000 in the red.

"She simply had no idea what she was doing," Orange said. "She spent and spent and spent."

To top it off, she had siphoned nearly a million dollars from the dealership account, funding the boutique and her own shopping sprees.

"She's robbing you blind," the accountant said. "You should go to the police."

"I'll take care of it," Shellard said. "Let me handle it."

Shellard began to take action. He informed his bank that he wanted Shirley removed as the signatory for his automotive dealership. Then he called a meeting with his friend, Eugene Hand and his lawyer Stuart Winston

"She's ripping me off," Shellard said. "The bitch is robbing me blind. She shuttled over $150,000 into her own account."

"You need to call the police," Winston said.

"I'm going to sell her house," Shellard said. "Fuck her. I need to recoup that loss."

Shellard then confronted Shirley about stealing his money. He was livid, demanding to know what she had been doing.

"He obviously felt betrayed," Orange said. "He was crazier than a shithouse rat, but let's face it, the guy had been good to her. He bought her everything she wanted and let her join him in this decadent lifestyle. But it wasn't good enough for her. She stole his credit cards. Wrote checks in his name payable to her."

Shirley didn't feel remorse at the dressing down by Shellard. She just didn't want the gravy train to leave.

THAT MONEY AIN'T GOING NOWHERE

Shirley began looking for a solution. She noticed a scraggly, down and out woman visiting her boutique often and a light bulb went on her head.

The woman was named Sophia.

Sensing she was a person with some wrong side of the street connections, Shirley saw Sophia and her boyfriend Stanley as "useful idiots" in a plot to kill her husband. They were low-level drug dealers willing to do anything for a buck.

Even if it included murder.

"Shirley gave them a song and dance about how she was an abused spouse," Orange said. "She told the two junkies that she had to endure nightly beatings and rapes. How Shellard would tie her up and have his way with her."

Sophia and Stanley, despite being heroin addicts and petty criminals, felt moral indignation.

Then Shirley waved a few thousand dollars in their face and they were willing to do whatever she asked.

On May 6th, 2005, Shirley lead the two junkies into Shellard's home.

"He's sound asleep in his bed until Shirley attacks him, placing a pillow case over his head," Orange said. "The two junkies hold Shellard down but he begins to fight. He struggles with Sophia and bites her finger. The junkie screams and takes some kind of heavy object from the bedside table and smashes Shellard over the head with it."

Shellard is knocked unconscious but that is when Shirley goes to work.

She takes a needle and injects him with heroin as she wants to make everything look like an overdose.

Then they pulled down his pants.

"Shellard is starting to come to," Orange said. "Then they shove a suppository up his rectum. Oxycontin. This coupled with the heroin is a powerful mix as he has a heart condition. A knock on the head, a shot of heroin and some Oxycontin shoved up his ass killed the man."

Peter is left for dead as Shirley lets some time pass before she calls the police.

A BAD ACTRESS AND A PAIR OF BUNGLING CRIMINALS

Shirley then conjures up her best Meryl Streep act as she calls the police and tells them that she has found Shellard dead on the floor.

"He was into rough sex," she blubbered. "I don't know who could have done this to him."

Police arrived and found the dead Shellard with a towel covering his genitals. His ankles were handcuffed and he was wearing a mouth gag. He also had dog leads, electrical cords and ropes tied around him.

Unfortunately for Shirley, however, the two junkies she hired were not exactly professionals.

A fingerprint sweep led police to Sophia.

Her print had been found on a hallway telephone. They would also find her DNA on a partially smoked cigarette in the kitchen.

The police would track down Sophia as well as her junkie boyfriend. They both confessed to the crime.

"I did it," Stanley said the moment he took a seat in the interrogation room. "Well, I should say that I helped them do it. Shirley drove me and Sophia to the mansion. She wanted him tied up because he had forced her to do bondage with him. Bondage! The dude had frozen all her accounts and was trying to sell her house behind her back. She told him that she wanted to sign some papers so that she could get her house back."

Stanley described the evening of the killing as a casual night on the town. He stated that Shirley took Sophia and himself to a hotel for some gambling.

"We played the poker machines," Stanley told the police. "Then we got some heroin and went to the mansion. Shirley had a syringe of heroin. She went into his bedroom and stuck him with it."

Shellard's daughters, all decent young women, were in shock at what happened to her father. Shirley took it upon herself to try and comfort Jenny but didn't mince words about the kind of man he was.

"Your father was into bondage," Shirley said to her after she tried to sell the police on the fact that Shellard's death was likely due to rough sex. "We never hurt each other, though."

"After my dad died, I confided in Shirley for support," Jenny said. "I thought that she would be the only one who could possibly understand the pain I was going through because she was going through it too."

Shirley didn't know that while she was talking daily on the phone with Jenny, the police had her phone tapped.

They would find out that Shirley was calling around asking for a hitman.

Setting up a sting, they assigned an undercover officer for the operation.

A HITMAN COMETH

Shirley made it known that she was looking for someone to "off" both Sophia and Stanley, thereby getting rid of her only witnesses.

An undercover officer, code-named "Victor" called Shirley and set up four meetings.

"Can you get me pictures of them?" Victor asked.

"No," Shirley said. "But I can get you their address."

"What do they do for a living?"

"They don't 'do' anything," Shirley scoffed. "They're fucking junkies. They sit around all day and shoot heroin."

"Why do you want them killed?"

"They were responsible for killing my husband," Shirley said. "I want them both taken care of."

"It will cost you ten thousand dollars," Victor said. "I need three grand up front. Down payment."

"No problem."

"I need you to get as specific as you can," the hitman said. "Do you want it to be quick or do you want them to suffer?"

"Yes," Shirley said, her eyes cold.

"But do you want them dead?" the hitman asked again. "Or in a wheelchair for the rest of their lives?"

"I want them both dead," Shirley said with finality. "Dead."

Shirley would be arrested and charged with Shellard's murder while the two junkies would receive six years in jail for manslaughter.

In 2007, however, Shirley would elect to go to trial. In her appeal, she somehow convinced the judge that she didn't mean to kill Shellard. She only meant to teach him a lesson.

Shirley would be sentenced to thirteen years in prison which could be lessened to nine years with good behavior.

At the time of this writing, Shirley has become eligible for parole.

A FINAL BETRAYAL

The story took another turn for the bizarre when trustees of Vera Moore's estate would claim that millions of dollars that Moore gave Shellard were meant as a loan and not a gift.

They argued that it should be repaid.

Moore had died eight years prior to Shellard being murdered. He had been a good friend of her son, Kenneth, who died in a car crash in 1972.

Moore then took a shine to the young Shellard, treating him as if he were her own son.

She would give him her son's Waring Bros Tourer Rolls-Royce. In return, Shellard would keep the elderly widow company. He would take her out of her suburban nursing home and drive her around in the Rolls-Royce while they would go out for tea.

"By all accounts," Orange said. "He seemed to have been good to her. Like a son. He was soon given the power of attorney for her and looked after her financial affairs."

Shellard would purchase the Rosecraddock mansion in 1984 for $1.4 million. This was done with Moore's money as the title was split between her company, Brenchley Gardens, and Shellard's company then called "Landro."

Shellard would always seem to have bad luck with women, not only while alive but in death as well as even the attorneys for his mother figure in Vera Moore would turn on him.

SHE DEVIL: THE TRUE STORY OF MYRA HINDLEY

ELLEN THOMAS

In the early 1960s, Myra Hindley took her first job out of school at a small chemical company called Millwards Merchandise. A shy eighteen-year-old, she kept to herself, reading in the office courtyard during breaks.

But she only did this to attract her co-worker, Ian Brady.

Brady would spend his breaks reading books. Myra soon followed suit in the hopes that he would approach.

After several months, the Glasgow, Scotland native finally made his move.

They both worked at the office as clerks. Brady was four years older than her as they began to date.

Myra lived with her grandmother and gave her virginity to the awkward co-worker on her grandmother's sofa. She would soon become Brady's accomplice in some of the most gruesome child killings in the history of Great Britain.

A BAD NEWS CHARACTER

Brady already had a police record for petty theft. He also had a strange demeanor, tilting his head oddly at people as he stared them down with hooded eyes.

He was nicknamed "Lassie", not a reference to the Collie dog but to his feminine body language. Brady was tall, skinny and would indicate later that he was a bisexual. As a child, he had few friends and was called "Dracula" in the neighborhood. He would torture kittens and see how long it took for them to die.

They were both bookworms and Brady would give Myra books on the Marquis De Sade, trying to introduce her to the world of sexual sadism. After their dates, he would invite her back to his place and play back recordings of Adolph Hitler's speeches.

The young couple would come up with pet nicknames for each other. Myra would call Ian "Hetty" after a character in the Goons and he would call her "Hess" after Hitler's deputy. They would soon become inseparable, both strangely odd people that felt that were superior and set apart from everyone else.

It soon became clear, however, that Ian was influencing Myra and not the other way around. He was her guide to the world of sexual sadism and then later, slowly revealed his desire to rape and murder children.

He started this by sharing a book in the same way he introduced her to sadomasochism. The book had detailed the "crime of the century". A child was the victim and one of the characters was named Myra.

"He had given me a book called 'Compulsion,'" Myra recalled. "Which was the story of Leopold and Loeb. They decided to commit the perfect murder. They were studying the philosophy of Nietzsche, his theory of the superiority of the pure Aryan and the strong overcoming the weak. It was very much the Nazi philosophy. They kidnapped a twelve-year-old boy for a ransom. They killed him, were caught and sent to prison. I told him it was a very disturbing book. But why exactly had he wanted me to read it? He told me he wanted to do a perfect murder and I was going to help him. That was why he needed me to pick someone up as I was a woman and a child would be more trusting of a woman. I burst into tears and he slapped my head backward and forward. I managed to fight him off and told him to stop it."

Myra fell prey to Ian's system of push and pull psychology. He would be abusive to Myra then inexplicably turn around and be sweet to her.

"I must be totally honest and say he wasn't always cruel and sadistic towards me," Myra said. "We had some pleasant times in country places that he'd found during his travels on his bike. We'd pack a picnic lunch, lots of coffee, bottles of wine and spend whole days in peace and tranquility. That was such a contrast to the other side of him. These were moments I treasured and thought about when things were bad. Trying to remember, telling myself that he couldn't help what he was and maybe in time he would become accustomed to ordinary domesticity and we could live a normal life."

IDLE HANDS

"Myra was a bored English girl looking for some adventure," forensic psychologist Paula Orange said. "Brady had an edge about him. Myra liked that about him, she wanted out of her dull life and into a world of edgy darkness, if you will."

Myra didn't judge Brady for being an avowed Nazi. She thought he was just going through a phase but he continued to play Richard Wagner's music full blast and storm around the house dressed up in Nazi regalia. Working himself up into a frenzy, he would then play rough sex games with Myra.

Myra found this aspect of Brady's personality to be alluring. She enjoyed dressing up in leather and black stockings, indulging whatever fantasy Brady could come up with.

"She was a sheltered young woman," Orange said. "And Brady opened up a whole new world to her. Think of it as 'Fifty Shades of Grey' with some Nazism thrown in and you have the whole relationship of Myra Hindley and Ian Brady."

The kinky sex continued and Brady gave stronger indications that he wanted to commit the perfect murder.

He wanted to harm children.

But he needed an accomplice.

"We can make the case that Myra made the jump from sadomasochistic sex to murder out of an obligation to Ian," Orange said. "It gave her a rush, to follow his lead. She needed more and more to get that same high."

The two would feed off each other sexually after which Ian would begin to plot the murders out. Who would be their victim? How would they kill them? Where would they kill them? He wrote things out in advance to the most minute detail.

"She (Myra) became desperate to fulfill his fantasies, his needs," journalist Clint Entwhistle said. "She was frightened, I suspect, of rejection by him."

So Myra didn't report him. She went along with his program.

SNAPPED

Brady had made his decision that they were going to kill someone. The night before, he took Myra to a bar on the back of his motorcycle. The two parked a little beyond the pub itself. Ian then began to intimidate Myra. He was jealous that she took a ride home from a co-worker.

"All the time we were talking," Myra recalled. "He was running a knife across his fingers. I honestly thought he was going to stab me. Then he laughed, put the knife away, told me never to accept a lift (the co-worker) again, and we drove back to the pub."

"Later as we were driving home, I dreaded what he would do when we got there, for I knew he would do something. "He raped me anally, urinated inside me and, whilst doing so, began strangling me until I nearly passed out. Then he bit me on the cheekbone, just below my right eye, until my face began to bleed. I tried to fight him off strangling me and biting me, but the more I did, the more the pressure increased. Before he left, when he'd seen the state of my face, he told me to stay off work the next day ..."

This would all take place under the roof of Myra's grandmother who was asleep when the assault took place.

"My gran almost fainted when she saw me and went to get my mother, who asked me if 'He' had done that to me. My mother disliked him intensely and kept telling me he was no good for me; she'd been telling me that since I'd met him at 18 and a half, but what girl of that age listens to her mother when she is wholly infatuated and in love? I told them what he had told me to say (she had been hit by a beer bottle during a bar fight) but I knew they didn't believe me."

THE FIRST MURDER

The following night after he beat down Myra, Brady selected his first victim.

He spotted a teenage girl walking to a dance by herself. She wore a sky blue jacket over a button-down red polka dot dress. Her white gloves and high heels turned on Ian Brady but what really arrested his attention was her face.

Cute with an air of innocence. A face that had an easy vulnerability, someone who would crack under the pressure of his whip.

Her pain and tears would be delicious, Ian thought.

Her name was Pauline Reede.

Brady gave Ian her orders and told her to pick the girl up. He would follow them on his bike.

"Ian Brady was awkward," Entwistle said. "He was not the kind of person a child would trust. There is no way anyone would have gotten into a car with him."

That is what he needed Myra for.

Myra did as he said, driving up alongside Pauline as she walked on the deserted road. The two young woman had already known each other from around the neighborhood.

"Can I give you a lift?" Myra asked.

"Oh, thank you, sure," Polly got into the small white van.

"Where are you going?"

"To the dance hall-"

"Okay," Myra said. "I just have to go to the Moors. I just lost one of my gloves. You can help me look for it. It will only take a second."

Pauline simply nodded her head. She trusted Myra.

THE KILLING FIELDS

"The Moors above Manchester were a special place for Ian Brady and Myra Hindley," Entwistle said. "They picnicked there together. They'd have sex there. It was a very, very important place to them."

It would also be the place where they would commit their first murder together.

Myra stepped off the van and directed Polly to look through some bushes. It was dark and Pauline asked if they should just look for it in the morning. Myra laughed it off and walked away, feigning as if she were looking for her gloves.

Ian Brady waited in the bushes, his mouth dry with anticipation, as he watched the sixteen-year-old Polly sift through the bushes.

Sneaking behind his victim, he slammed her across the head with a shovel.

Pauline Reede fell to the ground, stunned.

She would then be raped, tortured then murdered by the sadistic Brady.

"Brady was a sadist," Orange said. "He got off on the suffering of his young victim. The more innocent she was, the more she screamed, the more she pleaded for her life, the more he got off. It was part of the high for him. He had moved beyond the bedroom thrills with Myra and needed a bigger high. He wanted his fantasy to become reality."

Brady assaulted Pauline until she lost consciousness.

No longer able to provide him the "fun" of listening to her suffer, he took a knife to her throat and killed her.

Myra watched in silence as Ian Brady commit the brutal crime and then proceeded to bury Polly in a shallow grave.

"He led me to her body which I tried not to look at," Myra wrote. "I didn't know at the time that he was testing me at there was no need for me to be there. He told me to look at here. I'll never be able to forget what I saw. I stood and looked at the dark outline of the rocks against the horizon of the dark sky. Three people died that night. Pauline. My soul. And God. No God would have let what had happened, happen."

On the surface, however, Myra didn't seem distressed about the murder. She went to work the following Monday as if nothing happened.

"You would think if she had any conscience left she would have gone to the authorities," Orange said. "But Myra had been dehumanized by that point. The daily rapes and assaults made her numb to everything."

Still, a part of her old self remained. The disappearance of Pauline Reade sent shockwaves throughout Manchester. Myra was reading the newspaper one day and noticed a personal column written by Pauline Reade's mother.

It read " Pauline, please come home. We're heartbroken for you."

"I began to cry," Myra recalled. "Rocking myself back and forth with the paper clutched to my chest. I didn't hear his bike, nor knew that he'd come into the house. He asked me what was wrong but I couldn't answer; I couldn't stop shaking and crying, for I was devastated about what had happened to Pauline, and for her mum and dad. I really liked Mrs. Reade and used to feel sorry for her because she had problems with her nerves and always looked as though she was on the edge of a breakdown. He grabbed the paper off me and soon saw what I'd seen."

"He put the bolt on the front door in case gran came back, did the same to the back door, and began to strangle me. Before I lost consciousness, I heard him remind me of what he'd said after Pauline's murder, and that threat still stood. After the first murder, as we were driving home, he told me that if I'd shown any signs of backing out, I would have finished up in the same grave as Pauline."

MYRA'S EARLY LIFE

As one would expect, Myra grew up in an abusive home.

Her parents engaged in daily shouting matches which she watched from behind her bedroom door.

Her father would routinely beat her mother, exposing Myra to sudden violence during her formative years. He was a competitive boxer who would also engage in weekend bar brawls.

"He used to beat her a lot," Entwhistle said. "Her father was a very, very powerful influence on her life. She had a tough personality type to start with. If you combine that with a violent childhood, a childhood where she was taught how to be violent, how to be aggressive, then you end up with an unusual personality type."

Myra hated her father and saw him as a bully. He would teach her to box, often hitting her across the head when she performed the techniques incorrectly.

"My father wielded total parental control," Myra said. "I rebelled against it. Fought against it. All my life until I was old enough to free myself from it. All his attempts to control me, even the successful ones were at great cost and were the result of bitter recriminations and often a hard physical punishment."

Myra's father would give her spankings without warning, leaving her buttocks bruised.

Once when she was bullied by a little boy and came home with bruises on her face, her father locked her out of the house. He told her to either face down the bully or he was going to beat her up himself.

"I set up the street to meet my persecutor," Myra recalled. "I quickly concentrated on whatDad had told me and showed me. As Kenny's hand came up, I shot up my left hand, fist bunched towards his head. As I predicted, both hands went up to protect his face and I lifted my right hand and slammed it into his tummy, hitting him hard. With a gasp, Kenny Holden's knees crumbled and before he could recover I slammed my left fist into the side of his head. Kenny was so heavily shocked he sat down heavily on the floor and burst into tears. I stood looking down at him triumphantly."

Myra saw a lot of her father in Ian Brady. Aggressive. Ultra-violent.

"Myra did what we call in psychology, 'transference,'" Orange said. "She saw in Ian what she saw in her father. She never got her daddy's love. So in her mind, she saw Ian as Daddy. She wanted Daddy's love and would do whatever Ian wanted. That was part of her cycle. Transferring a deep need for her father's love onto Ian. There is the strong possibility that had Myra never hooked up with Ian she would have never become a murderer. But the two of them together? Horrific results."

"The bringing together of Myra Hindley and Ian Brady," Entwhistle said. "Unleashed an appalling set of criminal acts."

POLLY IS STILL MISSING

The disappearance of Polly Reede sent the town of Manchester on edge. Things like that simply didn't happen there.

"The fact that children were being abducted and killed," Entwhistle said. "Was incomprehensible to the ordinary man and woman in the street."

Myra would soon find out that Ian's sexual fantasies were not limited to teenaged girls.

He wanted boys too.

Myra would again be a willing accomplice in procuring Ian's second victim. This time, it would be twelve-year-old John Killbride. Myra would befriend the young boy before bringing him to the Moors where he would be sexually assaulted by Brady and later killed.

"I had a terrible feeling something had happened to him," John Killbridge's mother recalled when her son didn't come home from school. "Because he wasn't the kind of boy who would leave home for any reason. He was quite happy and very pleasant, always singing and whistling and I just couldn't see him going anywhere with anyone. Unless it was in an innocent way, somebody wanting to do a job with him or something like that. He'd be enticed into a car that way."

Ian would take photos of the body and burial site. This would become part of their ritual, their ceremony. They would perform the murder then take photographs as if to mark the moment. Then they would return to the scene of the crime days after with their dog "Puppet" in tow. They would take more pictures and relive what took place only days earlier.

"He stopped me as I was walking (to take a picture)," Myra recalled. "And said to turnaround. Moved me about a bit. Told me to kneel down and look at 'Puppet' whose head was showing when he was still wrapped inside my coat. I now know, and knew quite soon afterward, that he photographed me virtually kneeling on John Killbride's grave."

AN INSATIABLE HUNGER

Four months had elapsed between the Pauline and John Killbride murders. But now Ian could not wait long. He ordered Myra to deliver another victim to the isolated Moors.

His name was Keith Bennett. An exuberant, trusting boy, Keith looked like the proverbial nerd with a gap-toothed smile and professorial eyeglasses.

"Keith was a cheeky little lad," Entwhistle said. "He liked to go out and have fun."

Trusting that Myra was taking him some place fun, the young Keith was ambushed by Brady who wrapped a cord around his neck.

Myra did her usual best to remain detached while the horrific attack took place.

"I hadn't wanted this to happen," Myra recalled. "I was tense and terrified. I tried to concentrate my mind miles away from where I was. Finally, after roughly what I think was a half an hour by which time dusk began to descend. I heard him whistle or call. When I stood up, he was waving me back down to the stream bed. Virtually nothing was said as we made our way back except for him saying the spade was hampering him and he'd have to hide it, which he did."

The twelve-year-old Keith, whose entire family was waiting for him at his grandmother's house, never showed up.

His entire family would be traumatized for life.

"I am a mother," Keith's mother, Winnie Johnson said. "It was my first lad and I've got to find him no matter what."

Keith Bennett's body was never found.

"I have nightmares," Johnson said. "I jump in my sleep. It's getting to me now. Because I just can't get him back."

Meanwhile, Myra and Ian would once again take mementos of their time together, taking photos of themselves along the Moors on Keith's fresh grave. Days later, the two would go to St. James Church for midnight mass.

"I retained a warm religious glow," Myra said. "And came out feeling warmed. Not so Ian who took a long swill of whiskey and went to the grave where he casually urinated."

RITUALS

The photos of their time together became an obsession for Ian Brady. He had an automatic camera where he would set the timer and pose for photographs with Myra. In a few of them, they would pose on top of the fresh graves with Ian playfully choking Myra.

"Myra and Ian would often return to the scenes of their crimes," Orange said. "They would take photos of themselves there and relive the thrill of committing the murders."

Over time, however, the photos would not be enough stimulation. They needed something better. Something more visceral.

Sounds.

Ian Brady decided he would record the audio of their next victim being tortured.

That next victim would be ten-year-old Leslie Ann Downey. Myra would befriend and abduct her from the county fairgrounds.

"They would take her back to their home," Entwistle said. "Where he photographed her and recorded her being tortured."

Ian Brady would listen to the audio tape over and over again, closing his eyes and remembering the horrific acts he committed.

Is is the murder of Leslie that Myra would refuse to talk about in interviews.

"There's a tape that isn't what people think it is," Myra said, trying to downplay her own sadism evident in the tapes. "But it's bad. I just hurt so much to think that I've been such a cruel bastard."

THE RUSH OF KILLING

Like a drug addict needing a bigger hit to get high, Brady needed more and more of a thrill for his next murder. He started to get sloppy whereas before his attacks were meticulously planned out.

His next victim would be Edward Evans.

"Edwards was sixteen, seventeen years old," Entwhistle said. "And he picked him up in a pub in Manchester."

This would be the first time Ian acted in tandem with Myra to obtain the victim. They enticed the young man to come over to their home and there were witnesses in the pub.

The couple also invited Myra's brother in law, Dave Smith to watch the carnage.

"Smith had no idea what was going on," Entwhistle said. "He walked into it totally cold, totally unaware and soon found out that he was involved in the most horrific scene with blood all over the place. A man's head being smashed in."

Smith was appalled, then called the police and told them of the killing.

Police arrived on scene within minutes. They discovered the mauled body of Edwards in a tub. Both Ian and Myra would be arrested.

"It is inexplicable as to why the couple would allow Dave Smith to witness the murder," Orange said. "A part of me thinks that it was part of increasing the thrill. The desire to share what they felt was a special moment with someone else."

A CHILLING DISCOVERY

Investigators would then scour the home, finding one unusual clue that would reveal the goings on of the couple now known in the papers as the Moors Murderers.

They found a left over luggage ticket.

The police would go to the central train station and matched the ticket with a suitcase. Inside, the found something they would never forget.

"They kept trophies in suitcases," Entwhistle said. "In there, of course, was the tape recording of Leslie Ann Downey and that proved what they'd done."

The police would play back the tapes. It churned their stomach to hear the tearful cries of Leslie Ann Downey plead for her life.

"You need to do what he says," Hindley screamed at the little girl. "I told you to shut your face!"

"I want to go home," the little girl pleaded.

"Quiet! Do you not speak English?"

The tape would be played for the jurors at the trial of the couple.

According to witnesses, you could hear a pin drop when they played the tape in court.

"Afterward there was a long, stony silence," Entwhistle said. "As people reflected on what they just heard."

DENIAL

Myra would maintain her own innocence of the murders and repeatedly state that she never witnessed any of the killings herself.

"My solicitor (defense attorney) told me they'd found the body of a child," Myra said. "Identified as Lesley Ann Downey, did I know anything about it? And I said 'No.' A week after that, I'm not sure, they found John Killbride's body and they charged me with, I think it was the murder of John Killbride. Yes, it was.They set me down behind a table and behind it was a large poster of John Killbride. 'Will you just identify these pictures or these photos and tell us if you seen them before.' I'd say, yes, and then they turned over the picture to another photo of the unearthed body of John Killbride."

The picture, Myra would state, made her cry.

LETTERS TO MOMMA

Myra would write her mother numerous letters before her trial. She would order her mother to destroy the letters after she read them but her mother thought otherwise. She would also tell her mother to keep the photographs of her and Ian to herself.

"Don't believe what they're saying about us," Myra wrote. "It is all lies."

But the mothers of all the victims didn't see it that way.

In court, they all had an opportunity to confront Myra.

"The worst part was being confronted by Mrs. West in the witness box," Myra recalled. "And I was looking at her as she was giving evidence and she saw me looking at her and she screamed across at me. 'How can you look at me?' And she called me every name under the sun."

It is at this point that Myra stated that she began to fully realize the gravity of her crimes.

"It suddenly hit me just what I'd done and I think he (Ian) sensed this," Myra said. "We were sitting next to each other and he just put his hand on my arm and squeezed my arm. And I turned around and looked at him, and he was telling me with his eyes to keep quiet."

The jury would find them guilty and in May of 1966 both would be sentenced to life in prison.

STANDING BY HER MAN

Myra refused to testify against Ian. There were some legal experts at the time who believed that if she gave evidence against Brady she would have walked free. But she didn't. She elected to take the punishment along with him.

Instead, she accepted her sentencing and continued to write her mother.

"Dear Mum," Myra wrote. "I knew that I would have to go to prison for some time for 'harboring'. But I didn't think it would be for this long. Ian is in prison, in the special wing. Poor thing, he sews mailbags during the day. He says it helps to pass the time quicker than expected. Will you do one thing for me, ma'am? Take out a policy on me or for me, for a half gram a week. I can't even begin to think of the future. It will be something to fall back on."

"Ian has got a little mouse in his cell. He feeds it crumbs and sits in bed watching it nibble them. The other night, he left it half a chip, thinking it wouldn't touch it but when he woke up the next morning it had disappeared."

Over the next three years, Myra would bombard her mother with requests for the photographs of her and Ian together. She said she did this at the behest of Ian who wanted both the slides and photographs desperately. Myra's mother eventually relented by was sure to allow the police copies of the negatives.

"Ian wanted those pictures back so bad because it reminded him of the events," Orange said. "That is the sort of thing we've come to expect from certain types of serial killers. They want to relive the moment in their fantasy. They'll take mementos, pictures, different elements of their crime in order so they can relive it in their minds. The pictures of Myra holding their dog on those burial sites were of paramount importance to Ian."

Myra would die in prison in 2002 of respiratory failure. Her ashes would be scattered over the Moors, a place that she loved so much.

"Was Myra Hindley sick or was she evil?" Entwhistle asked. "She had a violent father. She met a sexually sadistic man who desperately wanted to be a serial killer. All those things came together and made her carry out some evil, appalling crimes."

Ian Brady remains alive, living out his years under suicide watch in a psychiatric facility where he has repeatedly stated that he will kill himself if given the chance.

HUSBAND KILLER : THE TRUE STORY OF LARISSA SCHUSTER

ERIN EDWARDS

Larissa Leann Foreman was born January 1, 1960. She grew up on a farm near Clarence Missouri. By all accounts she had a happy childhood. She won first place at the Randolph pony show, her father, Charles, won first place in the men's division and Deeann, her mom, won second in the bareback for pleasure division. Her parents seemed to be very involved in her life. She excelled academically; she was athletic and went after what she wanted with everything she had. She was described as a 'go getter'.

Larissa graduated High school and went on to the University of Missouri Columbia to become a biochemist. She didn't come from a rich family so she would work as a nursing aide at Boone Hospital Center in Columbia Missouri. It's not known whether she liked her work as an aide, however she did like a nurse named Tim Schuster, and he liked her as well. She was electrifying and intoxicating, Tim was enthralled. They started dating after becoming friends and just hanging out together after work.

Finally, in 1982 Tim popped the question, and Larissa said yes. Between 1982 and the birth of their second child Tyler in 1990 there was a whirlwind of things happening. There was the wedding in '82, the birth of their first child, Kristin, and a move to sunny central California, Fresno to be exact.

In the beginning Tim managed the cardiology Department for St Agnes Medical Center. While Larissa worked for Pan Agricultural Laboratories. Larissa saw the company declining and thought it a good time to start her own company; Central California Research Lab. She was ambitious and worked long hours to make her company a success. Tim continued to work at St Agnes and be both Mom and Dad to their two children.

According to friends Bob and Mary Solis, Tim was the one who made sure doctor appointments were kept, homework was done and dinner was cooked and on the table. Larissa ruled her house and Tim having a non-confrontational personality went along with her, if for no other reason than to keep the peace. By this time she was making more than twice what Tim made. It was her money that made it possible for them to move to Clovis and buy a much larger home than the one they had in Fresno. It looked like they had it all...but did they?

By this time Kristen was a teenager and as with most teens there was attitude. Kristen fought with her mother at almost every turn. She stood up to Larissa in such a way that she felt she had no other option than to send her daughter to her parents in Clarence, Missouri. Tim was upset that his wife didn't even discuss this move with him; she'd decided this IS what will happen. And soon his beloved little girl was gone. But still Tim kept quiet.

The Schuster's entered into a bitter, rancorous separation in 2002, after nearly 20 years of marriage and two children. They tried living in the same house after the separation. However Larissa was not happy with this arrangement. From the very beginning she didn't want Tim to have anything to do with Tyler, no visitation and no kind of a relationship with his son at all. This was not okay with Tim. On more than one occasion she made the statement that she wished Tim would just die.

In late June or early July Larissa took Tyler and went on a trip out of state. Tim took this opportunity to secure a condo and move out of the family's home. Larissa was livid that he would have the nerve to leave while she was away and accused him of taking things from the house that didn't belong to him. What earlier seemed like idle threats became something more, she told a neighbor that she should just get it over with and kill Tim herself.

A Plan started formulating shortly after Tim moved out of the Clovis family home. Larissa asked James Fagone a lab assistant and Larissa's sometimes babysitter, sometimes whipping boy if he would help break in to Tim's house and help her get back somethings he took when he moved out. She felt he wasn't entitled to them and left messages on his answering machine telling him he'd better bring them back...or else.

After returning from a trip Tim came home to a house that had been burglarized and ransacked. One of the things missing...the very set of mixing bowls Larissa had had such a fit over. Who was her accomplice in the break-in...none other than James Fagone? Larissa wasn't shy about what they had done, she told her manicurist Terri Lopez, that after the break-in she would go back to Tim's house and sit in a chair and look around at what they had done. She also told Tami Belshay that "it gave her a feeling that was better than sex."

After the burglary the Schuster's relationship went even further downhill. Tim knew who had broken into his condo. Larissa's bitterness not only let her destroy things in the condo, but she even bragged about keying his truck. She said it made her happy every time she saw the marks on his truck. Tim seemed worried about what his estranged wife was capable of. He moved again, this time to a house in Clovis that had motion sensors and an alarm. He obtained a handgun and a permit to carry a concealed weapon. Larissa had told her manicurist Ms. Lopez that she prayed every night that Tim would just die. At one point Larissa told her that she could kill Tim and get away with it. She also asked one of the employees at CCRL if her boyfriend knew anyone that would kill Tim or at least rough him up. She'd made remarks like this before and all who heard them thought she was just venting because the divorce wasn't going the way she wanted it to. She said she would do anything to keep Tim from getting the business.

According to Bob and Mary Solis, Larissa would belittle and embarrass Tim in front friends and family alike. She seemed to relish the power she had over him.

In late June St Agnes let everyone know that there would be a round of layoffs coming and to be expecting it. Tim and his friend Mary Solis was on the short list to be let go. Larissa laughed when she heard the news. On July 9th Tim, Mary, her husband Bob and another friend Victor Uribe all had dinner together. The group broke up about 10pm that night, before Tim left the Solis' they had made arrangements to meet for breakfast the next morning. Tim never showed for his exit meeting or for breakfast. This worried Bob and Mary, it seems Tim was never late for anything, and if he thought he was going to be late he called. He was also supposed to pick up Tyler that evening.

His friends tried to reach Tim, calling his cell phone. Finally they called Uribe and told him that they couldn't reach Tim and would he go by the house and check on their friend. Uribe arrived at Tim's house and went inside. There didn't seem to be anything out of place, until he went to the bedroom. Tim's watch, wallet and cell phone were lying on the dresser. Uribe was now worried as well. Victor said "He never went anywhere without his cell, he kept it with him at all times, in case the kids needed him."

No one knew what had happened to Tim. The police refused to even take a missing person's report until he'd been missing 24 hours. July 10th when Tim had not been heard from in the allotted time Bob Solis filed the missing person's report. Officer John Willow from the Clovis Police Department responded to the call.

Willow found Tim's handgun under a cushion of a chair. He found Tim's cell phone in the bedroom and called all the numbers in his contacts to see if any of them had seen or heard from Mr. Schuster. When he called Larissa she said she hadn't heard from him either. He also talked to Terri Lopez and she relayed to Willow that the Schuster's were going through a rather nasty divorce. John Willow decided to turn the case over to Detectives Larry Kirkhart and Vincent Weibert.

When they entered Tim's home they noted some damage on the wall behind the chair where the gun was found earlier. They found a briefcase in the same room as the chair. Inside they found a microcassette recorder and tape. In the bedroom they found an answering machine that showed only one number, a cell phone number belonging to Larissa Schuster. Detective Kirkhart then asked Larissa to come to the police station for a chat about her missing husband.

During her interview with the detectives she told them that she and Tim were getting a divorce and that they did not communicate very well with each other. They asked her about her cell number being on the caller ID. She fabricated a story about being asleep on her couch and waking up to find she had pushed some buttons and maybe she had speed dialed Tim. They asked her if she had her phone with her and she said no. Kirkhart called for a pause in the interview and went to the parking lot to find Larissa's car. He looked in the window and saw a phone on the center console, dialed her number and the phone in the car rang.

Kirkhart went back to the interview room and asked Larissa to come with them to unlock her car and retrieve her phone. Back inside the station the interview resumed. The detective went through her contacts that she had on speed dial, none of them were Tim's number.

Larissa's whole demeanor changed, she was shaking and in the opinion of the detectives showing signs of deceit. She came clean and admitted that she had lied to the detectives and she knew she shouldn't have. She claimed she wasn't trying to be deceitful. None the less they let Schuster go home, for now. At this point in their investigation they still had no idea what had happened to Tim. Kirkhart had asked Larissa if she thought that Tim could just cash out some money and leave town, go camping or to Vegas to just get away. She told them she didn't think he would do that, that he wouldn't leave his son like that. This was still just a missing person case and most of Tim's friends thought that perhaps he had just had enough, the divorce, the custody battle, losing his job was to much for him to handle. Tami Belshay, Bob and Mary Solis and Victor Uribe were among those friends. The detectives were thinking the same thing at this point.

With no solid leads on Tim's whereabouts detectives Weibert and Kirkhart kept searching for some clue, however small that might give them some direction on finding Tim. Kirkhart was going through Tim's ledger provided to them by Larissa. And they came across a name they were familiar with...James Fagone. They knew his name because he was the one suspected of breaking into Tim's house with Larissa shortly after Tim moved out of the family home a year earlier. They also knew that he was an associate of sorts of Larissa's.

The following Monday Detectives Kirkhart and Daly called Fagone to come and talk with them. Vince Weibert thought that perhaps Fagone might have some "inside" information on Tim's disappearance.

It seems that Fagone was a babysitter for the Schuster's son Tyler, before and after their separation. James was a good kid according to his attorney Peter Jones. "He's an above average student, higher than a 4.0 grade point average...a gentle spirit."

Fagone was nervous during the police interview. He admitted that Larissa had him help her break into Tim's house and take back things that she didn't want him to have.

James told the detectives that Larissa was going around the house looking for things and he just wanted to get the TV and some other stuff so he wasn't paying attention to what she was doing. Obviously James was scared out of his mind by now, but they pressed him more telling him they "knew he was involved somehow" with Tim's disappearance. Fagone's determination not to tell what had happened, what him and Larissa Schuster had done crumbled.

Fagone confessed that he had been there the night that Tim went missing, that he had gone to his house with a weapon. James relayed to them that Larissa had paid him the $2000 to purchase a stun gun and that he could just keep the rest for himself.

So as the day wore on James conveyed the sordid details of the night in questions.

On the night that Tim lost his job at St Agnes and had dinner with a group of friends, James had done what he was told to do by Larissa, buy a stun gun. Later he would get the call from her (Larissa). She picked him up and went to Tim's house. James laid in wait in the darkness just outside of his door. He could hear Larissa on the phone telling Tim that Tyler wasn't feeling well and she needed him to come to the front door.

A few moments later Tim opened the front door and James sprung from the shadows and attacked him wrestling him to the ground. Tim was struggling; James was using the stun gun on him, on the arm at first, not sure where else he might have zapped him. Soon Tim stopped struggling and when James looked up he saw Larissa with a rag that had been soaked in chloroform.

Were the detectives hearing this right? Was Fagone confessing to the murder of Timothy Schuster? But if they were going to believe any of it they needed some kind of evidence. They asked about the stun gun again, and what had Fagone done with it. He told them he threw it in a portable toilet on the edge of town. The investigators found the stun gun, right where James told them it should be.

Now at the same time Fagone was being interviewed Clovis Police Department got a call from a woman saying that her boss ask her to do something that in retrospect seemed a little off, suspicious even. Her Boss...Larissa Schuster. Leslie Dodd had been instructed to rent a moving truck by her boss. She was told to use her personal credit card and rent it in her own name not her boss's. A year earlier Larissa had asked the same employee to rent a storage unit near Schuster's lab, again to do it in the employees name and with her personal credit card.

Jim Koch got the call to check it out. He went to the storage unit and walked down the hall. He had been told to look for a blue barrel. When he found Schuster's unit and opened the door "there was a very very strong odor." Koch said. "I had on a breathing apparatus and gloves."

He saw the blue barrel, he opened it.

Koch said in an interview, "And when I opened the barrel I—I saw something that was very, very shocking to me and I recognized immediately as human remains. There was a barrel that's over 3/4 of the way full of fluid and portions of—of—body protruding from the fluid. And the body was obviously decaying. It was placed in acid. And the acid was basically eating away at the body."

Had Larissa Schuster killed her husband and put him in the barrel? According to James Fagone, yes she had, and he had helped her and then watched as she poured a caustic solution in on top of Tim. Worst of all, Tim was probably still alive when the acid was poured on him and he was sealed inside the barrel.

Tim had been found, the truth had come out and the Clovis detectives were on their way to Missouri to arrest Larissa for the murder of her husband Tim. They met her at the airport where she had gone to see her family. According to the detectives that arrested her for the murder she didn't even ask what had happened to Tim or how he died.

Both James Fagone and Larissa Schuster were arrested and charged with 1st degree murder.

Now that the perpetrators of Tim Schuster's murder had been arrested it was time to take them to trial. The murder was committed in the early morning hours of July 10, 2003. There was a lot left to do before the trial could begin.

The Clovis police department had to finish gathering evidence, talk to friends and family to make sure that everything was done correctly. They wanted to make sure that Larissa and James would not be let go on a technicality.

The judge had to decide if he would make this a death penalty case or a life in prison without parole case. That would be decided later. The prosecutor had to prepare a rock solid case and present the evidence to a jury in a manner that would guarantee a conviction. The defense would also be talking to people on behalf of their clients. Find people that had nothing but good things to say about them in hopes of offsetting the horrible truths that would come out at trial.

The judge separated the cases and James and Larissa would be tried separately. James was tried first. His attorney portrayed James as a misguided man who hero worshipped Larissa.

He was found guilty and is now serving a life without parole sentence.

There was so much media coverage on Larissa that the defense asked and received a change of venue. Her trial was moved to Los Angeles.

Monday October 22, 2007 Larissa's trial started. Prosecutor Dennis Peterson relayed to the jury of 9 women and 3 men just how the murder went down. He told them that Tim was still alive when the acid was poured over him while he laid head first inside the blue barrel. Her motive? She didn't want to share anything that they built during their 19 ½ years of marriage. She felt Tim didn't deserve any part of the business, or home and didn't want him to have contact with their tween son, Tyler.

CCRL employees would also testify to the facts of the blue barrel being at the lab and the day Tim was reported missing went to look for it and it was gone. They also said that Larissa had said that she should just shove Tim in the barrel and get rid of him.

A large amount of Hydrochloric acid, 12 gallons and Sulfuric acid, 4 gallons was ordered for Schuster's lab, more than ever before. Leslie Dodd (nee Fichera) testified that, "that was more acid than the lab would use in a year."

Joseph Boatwright thought Larissa was joking when she asked "if he thought a body would fit in the blue barrel."

Juror's watched several hours of Larissa's police interview. She made Tim out to be controlling and having a volatile temper. After seeing that part of the interview Bob Solis testified to the contrary, that Tim was very calm and a non-violent, non-confrontational person.

In another part of the interview with Clovis Detectives Schuster stated that "she prayed that Tim would get over this hostility about the divorce." Her manicurist Terri Lopez told a different story. Lopez said that "she told me she prayed every night he would die."

A hair stylist Becky Holland sometimes did Larissa's hair. During those appointments Larissa would rant about Tim. Holland didn't think much about it because she knew they were going through a divorce. Later though she said the hateful remarks escalated, Holland told the court, "this is getting a little creepy. It was so intense."

The jurors got to hear just how intense it was when they got to hear message after message of Larissa calling her husband awful names and making threats about their children. The prosecutor used these recordings to make a point to the jury; Larissa was in a "murderous rage". Nuttall interjected that these messages were left on Tim's machine 7 months before the murder.

And with this the prosecution rested, hoping that they had proved their case. There was one witness that they really needed to be able to lockdown the case against Schuster, they needed James Fagone. The judge had barred his confession so the jury would never hear in his own words what happened July 10, 2003. But he refused to cooperate with Peterson because he had already filed his appeal. The only thing that might have helped Peterson is the fact that James Fagone had already been convicted of Tim's murder.

Nuttall began the defense's case by telling the jury that neither he nor his client could tell them what had happened to Tim because "we don't know". And since the jury heard nearly nothing about Fagone, Roger Nuttall blamed the murder on him. After all Fagone had already been found guilty of the murder Larissa was now on trial for. Nuttall said in his opening statements that "Tim was an angry man who belittled Larissa in over-compensation for his own failings as a husband and father." And that "he began stalking Larissa after the divorce proceedings started."

Now Defense attorney Nuttall brought in a stream of witnesses that would steer the blame away from his client.

He had a medical expert that said the victim's body was cut in half and that the police had completely missed a second crime scene and the evidence from there would have proved that Fagone and others were responsible for Tim's murder not Larissa.

Nuttall even had psychiatrist Stephen Estner on the stand. Estner said that, "My impression was that Mrs. Schuster was a very direct and assertive person, and Mr. Schuster was a more passive and nurturing personality. And I think they started butting heads over that."

Larissa Schuster took the stand in her own defense and adamantly denied the charges saying, "No, I did not kill my husband." Again James Fagone would have the whole murder put squarely on him. Schuster told the jury, ""I heard him say something like 'there had been an accident and Tim is dead.' I thought he was joking."

She said that the $2000 payment to Fagone was for babysitting Tyler and housesitting while she was away on vacation with her son. Schuster said the large amount of acid was for cleaning a large scale of lab glass. Schuster seemed to explain everything away poking holes in the prosecutor's case. Would it be enough to get an acquittal? Had she actually swayed the jury?

It seemed that the trial was plagued with problems, including accusations of juror misconduct. At least one juror was replaced by an alternate due to disruptive behavior. Another admonished for giving Larissa a 'thumbs up' after her testimony. And yet with all of that...it was time for the jury to deliberate of the weeks of testimony they'd heard.

It took a little more than two days for the jury to decide on a verdict.

Guilty of Murder with a special circumstance of financial gain. The verdict came exactly one year after Fagone's.

Roger Nuttall slowed the sentencing of Larissa Schuster while he tried to find reasons to ask for a new trial. He even used the argument that there may have been juror misconduct. Nuttall wanted to talk to the jurors but Ellison said no. Nuttall appealed and the District court of Appeals told Ellison to contact the jurors on Schuster's behalf. All the jurors and alternates refused to speak to her attorney.

So on May 8, 2008, five months after being found guilty of her estranged husband's murder Larissa Leeann Schuster was sentenced to life in prison without the possibility of parole. Judge Ellison also denied her request for a new trial.

At the sentencing a total of seven people stood up to make statements about how they had been affected by the murder of Timothy Allen Schuster.

Kristen, Tim and Larissa's oldest child and only daughter made an emotionally charged statement to and about her mother.

She called her mother a demon for "taking my father away." And told her. "I pray you're continually haunted at night by the sight and sound of my father fighting for his last breathing moments on this earth. I hope you toss and turn and have horrible nightmares visualizing the horrific act of violence you have committed. Maybe later in life I can learn to forgive you, but I doubt it. This is goodbye, not just for now, but forever. This is goodbye as your daughter."

Kristen was so devastated over her father's murder she reached out to a support group murdervictims.com. Several people shared their own experiences of losing a parent at a young age hoping she could find at least a little peace.

SHAYNE LOVERA

133

KIM RILEY

The life of Alicia Shayne Lovera looked like something out of a soap opera.

Born into poverty, she was ushered into a life of wealth and privilege when her mother married a rich president of a bank. She grew up to be beautiful, popular and spoiled. But she soon find herself in financial ruin when her stepfather committed suicide, leaving the family with nothing.

Her sense of entitlement still intact, she married a struggling math teacher who couldn't resist her charms.

But when the marriage became an inconvenience, she did what all black widows do.

She killed her husband.

This is her story.

EARLY LIFE

Alicia Shayne Good was born in 1966 to teenage parents. Going by her middle name Shayne, her early life wasn't easy as her parents lacked the necessary resources to provide. Her mother would divorce her father. But when Shayne turned seven-years old things to a turn for the better.

"Her mother and she were poor," journalist Jamie Satterfield said. "Her mother met Brent Mills who was a bank president and they married into that family and Brent adopted Shayne."

The change in life circumstance was jarring to the young Shayne. She was instantly given an upgrade in lifestyle as she the world was now her oyster. There were expensive vacations, cars and garish parties.

Her new stepfather, Brent Mills, was a bank executive who treated Alicia and her mother Sandy to all the spoils his job could bring. He was well regarded in the business community and had several contacts.

But Brent had inherited the bank built by his father and lacked his business acumen. He was lenient in granting loans and the bank soon grew insolvent. He was also suspected of using the bank as a money laundering service for drug dealers.

On the surface, Brent told the family that the allegations were all fraudulent. He gave them every assurance that everything would be okay.

Then he killed himself.

"He took a gun to his head and blew his brains out," forensic psychologist Paula Orange said. "That left an indelible image on Shayne's outlook on life."

His suicide would leave the family in financial ruin. The papers would ridicule Mills, giving voice to all of the wild allegations of his mismanagement. The family would be left shamed and with nothing.

The effect was devastating on Shayne. She would go from being the richest girl in the school to being dirt poor.

Again.

Shayne just wanted to get away. She had entertained aspirations of being broadcast anchor, thinking that her beauty and speaking skills would lead to an easy gig. So she decided to move out of state for college. She would attend a university in Missouri where she would meet Kelly Lovera.

They would marry a year later.

The couple would have two children over the next five years despite being the polar opposites temperamentally.

Kelly was cool, calm and wanted a quiet life. He didn't embrace the partying lifestyle that Shayne wanted.

"Theirs was a union that is hard to comprehend," Orange said. "Kelly was not en route to becoming the next bank president. He was a twenty-year old student who was struggling. He wanted to be a math teacher. Shayne wanted to live a hedonistic lifestyle. She wanted to party and spend lavishly. Why they would get married defies explanation."

Bored in Missouri, Shayne would then convince Kelly to move back to her hometown in Tennessee. Kelly would consent to the move.

A RETURN TO POVERTY

The couple would live in Sevierville which was thirteen miles north of her former luxury home in Gatlinburg. But it was light years away in terms of affluence as they were forced to rent out a small, one story townhouse.

The neighborhood they lived in was called "Frog Alley".

"A luxury once experienced becomes a necessity," Orange said. "Shayne had gotten used to living the high life. But married life, particularly one with of a lack of resources, would prove to be difficult for her."

"Frog Alley was a place for the working poor," Satterfield said. "To come back and live there would be extremely embarrassing for her."

Kelly's focus was not on making money. He was working on his master's degree in mathematics while he took a teaching position at Pellissippi College in Knoxville. Shayne would work various odd jobs to help the family make ends meet and was not happy about that.

"She had wild ambitions to become a news anchor," Orange said. "But she didn't do anything to make that happen. She wanted someone else to do all the work for her just like she experienced when her step-father financed her life."

BOREDOM SETS IN

Shayne entertained neighbors for barbecues and poker nights. The problem is, the only people that seemed to come around were other men.

She was thoroughly bored with her marriage and began to have multiple affairs.

"She would flirt with men in full view of the children," Orange said. "Men would come over ostensibly to play cards. She would play 'footsie' with them underneath the poker table. She didn't want to be a mother and got bored with that act. She wanted to party, to be the rich wild girl that she was as a teenager. The idea of staying home with a boring math teacher and two needy children was anathema to her. She wanted a way out."

The affairs would occur in her apartment when Kelly was away. Different men would come and go at various hours.

"He's (Kelly) cramping my style," Shayne told one of her lovers. "And you're so much better than him."

"Thanks," her lover said with a grin.

"Do you know anything about how to poison someone?"

"Excuse me?"

"You know," Shayne said. "How certain poisons are undetectable."

Shayne would test the waters with her lovers. She would ask them about poisons in a joking manner. But then they would soon realize that she was serious. There was an ulterior motive to her affairs.

She wanted to find someone to kill her husband.

And she would find a willing assassin in Brett Rae.

THE NEXT DOOR NEIGHBOR

Brett was young and inexperienced with women. He had never encountered anyone like the sexy Shayne Lovera.

"Brett fell very hard for Shayne," Satterfield said. "Their affair started very quickly. And it was hot and heavy."

"Brett was a rich kid," Satterfield said. "His father was a newspaper publisher (Rick Rae, a Canadian publisher of the Sevier County newspaper). He was a well-to-do guy. He was just wild. He was just one of those people who was 'full-on' all of the time. He was up for anything."

And he was completely infatuated with Shayne.

Shayne set up Brett the same way she set up her other lovers. After a torrid session of lovemaking, she popped the question.

Will you kill my husband?

"I'll do anything for you," he told her with baited breath.

Shayne offered him a deal.

"If he were to get rid of Kelly," Satterfield said. "Then he would get her. That's what Brett wanted."

"Brett let his little head do the thinking for his big head," Orange said. "He was going to inherit money from his father so he had absolutely nothing to gain by killing Shayne's husband. Nothing except sex which of course if he had money, he would have more options than a narcissistic married woman. He simply did not have the life experience to see Shayne for what she was."

She would have a party on November 5th, 1994, an outdoor barbecue with gambling and drinking. Kelly left the party early and went to sleep on the couch.

Brett would be the last one to leave that evening. On his way out the door, they both noticed Kelly asleep on the couch.

"It was a spontaneous thing," Orange said. "They didn't have a murder weapon so they used whatever was immediately available. That would be the baseball bat of Kelly's son."

Kelly would then be bludgeoned to death.

"The plan was to put him in his own vehicle," Satterfield said. "And make it look like an accident."

Brett then dragged Kelly into his jeep and drove down Highway 14. He parked near an embankment and pushed the jeep down the side, watching it carom into a tree.

He then called one of his friends to pick him up.

Brett did not keep the news of the murder to himself. He would brag to two of his friends of what he had done.

"I put him (Kelly) over a hundred foot embankment," Brett said. "I fucked his wife and killed his ass. She told me I'd get more sex and more money if I get rid of him so I did."

Brett told his friends of the other methods he thought of using to kill Kelly but that he decided to beat him to death with the baseball bat then "stage a car crash."

FINDING THE BODY

A pair of tourists would discover Kelly's black jeep below the road. Inside, they would see his bloodied dead body. Initially, they

believed that he was the victim of an accident. They called the authorities and reported that it appeared as if his jeep had gone off the road and hit a tree

Park Ranger Jerry Grubb was notified of the "accident" at the Great Smoky Mountains National Park.

The whole scene, however, looked suspicious from the get-go.

"Just wasn't any skid marks," Grubb said. "No disturbed gravel. There just wasn't any disturbance in that area."

Grubb looked inside the jeep and found the body of Kelly Lovera, laying in a pool of blood trailing toward the front seat. The blood should have been trailing behind the victim if he had, in fact, struck the tree head on.

Additionally, Kelly's injuries were not consistent with a car crash victim. The facial injuries appeared to be the result of a beating, not the impact of the jeep against the tree.

MURDER ON THEIR HANDS

The autopsy would reveal that Kelly had been beaten to death and a homicide investigation ensued. Authorities would then visit Shayne's apartment and inform her of her husband's death.

She would go into hysterics, sobbing uncontrollably.

"Do you know why anyone would want to do this to him?" an investigator asked.

"He doesn't have any enemies!" she bawled.

But an officer would notice blood splatter on the glass of Kelly's diploma that was placed on a wall near the couch. They would obtain a search warrant and a crime team would arrive, spraying luminol over the apartment.

Luminol lightens up blood stains when a fluorescent ray is scanned over it.

"The whole living room lit up like a Christmas tree," Orange said. "That is when they knew they had the guilty party."

Detectives then began to question neighbors who all pointed their fingers at Brett Rae, the lover of Shayne.

Both Shayne and Brett were arrested and charged with first-degree premeditated murder.

Brett would confess quickly. He admitted to using the baseball bat and then staging the car wreck. He would be represented by Robert Ritchie who would prep him for the murder trial for nearly three months. Ritchie, however, would notice that Brett was completely obsessed with Shayne. He then turned the case over to Robert Ogle but two weeks before the trial Alan Feltes was brought in as Brett was given joint representation.

"His attorneys were flabbergasted at his refusal to give up Shayne," Orange said. "He was truly in love with her and wanted to protect her even if it meant incriminating himself."

"I did it," Brett insisted. "Just leave her out of it."

Feltes told Brett that there was no way he could win the case with all of the evidence stacked against him. The only thing Brett cared about was putting Shayne in jeopardy.

THE TRIAL

Park Ranger Jerry Grubb would testify against the killing duo, presenting the forensic evidence found at the home and jeep. Friends and family would testify that both Shayne and Brett had bragged to them about what they had done.

Going in desperation mode, Shayne would then take the stand. She wanted to tell her version of what happened that night.

"Brett had stopped by to talk to me when Kelly came out and confronted him," Shayne said. "They began fighting and Brett picked up a baseball bat. He swung it only to keep Kelly away. But then he accidentally hit him and killed him."

Shayne would go on to say that she didn't witness any of this. She was asleep and really knew nothing that happened.

"Brett and I were not lovers," Shayne said. "We were nothing more than neighbors. It was a case of fatal attraction. He had a thing for me and wanted to kill my husband."

She didn't know, however, that when both she and Brett were released on bail they were followed by a Siever County Sheriff. He followed them into the mountains and saw them having intercourse in the woods.

When Shayne was confronted with this evidence, she tried to regroup.

"I had sex with Brett," Shayne said. "But only because I had to. He threatened to involve me in the murder plot. My purpose in going there was trying to save what little bit of life I had left at that point."

The explanation did not go over well with the jury. It took them only an hour and a half to return with a guilty verdict.

OFF TO JAIL

On January 29th, 1996, both Shayne and Brett would be convicted of Kelly's murder. They would not be given the death penalty, however. The prosecution wanted a sentence of life without parole.

Feltes approached by the attorneys for Shayne. They stated that a plea agreement would be possible but it would have to be a package deal with Brett.

Feltes advised Brett to take the deal as the plea agreement would guarantee him a life sentence with possibility of parole. If he didn't take the deal, the odds would be that he would be facing life without parole.

"Just don't do anything to hurt Shayne," Brett said. "I want to see her."

"What?"

"I want to see her before I take the deal."

Brett would persist in wanting to see Shayne. Instead he would take the deal.

"His attorneys described him as having the saddest eyes they had ever seen in a courtroom," Orange said. "He was truly in love with

Shayne. She, on the other hand, threw him under the bus. She was willing to say whatever it took to get herself off and it backfired."

THE AFTERMATH

Kelly's children would be placed into the care of his parents. Brett and Shayne would receive life with parole after twenty-five years.

Brett would later try to appeal his sentencing despite agreeing to a plea bargain which barred him from doing so.

His claim would be rejected.

Ray would write that "his trial was ineffective for encouraging him to accept the state's offer of life with possibility of parole; failing to prepare for mitigating circumstances at the sentencing phase; failing to properly conduct a pre-trial investigation; failing to adequately consult with him during critical stages of the proceedings; failing to advise him of his rights to direct appeal and collateral attack of his conviction; deficient performance of counsel at trial; his guilty plea was coerced and involuntary; and his conviction is void as violating the protection against double jeopardy."

"He had conceded his guilt during the guilty plea hearing and that his attorneys did the best they could...he made these admissions only because the attorneys instructed him to do so and although he agreed that he believed himself to be guilty of first degree murder at the time of his plea, he now retracts that admission."

Brett's attorney Feltes would dispute his allegations, stating that he "never had any problem with Brett being incoherent or not understanding anything he was told or advised."

Both Brett and Shayne remain in prison, waiting to be paroled in 2025.

SAMANTHA SCOTT

ROBERTA NEWELL

Andrea Claire aka Samantha Scott had was born in 1941 and grew up in New Jersey.

At the age of 15, Andrea claimed that her mother forced her to marry the man who got her pregnant. In Andrea's words, she was rape but according to her mother, the 22-year old man got Andrea drunk and "took advantage." The man was a friend of her sister and reportedly was either set up on a date with her or picked her up from basketball practice.

Known to her friends as "Drea," Andrea would divorce the man after over two volatile years of abuse but the union still produced two children. Armed with only a 9th grade education, Andrea had no skill set and bounced from job to job. She began working as secretary, waitress, escrow worker, model and touring exotic dancer.

CAROUSEL OF MEN

She married again in a union that lasted three days as her new husband didn't want her to bring her children into the marriage (she met him while setting a trap to find out who was stealing her morning newspaper.) Her third marriage was to a Jordanian national who needed a wife in order to stay in the U.S.

"I married for a third time to a young Jordanian student," she said. "He had cousins in countries that he was afraid he'd be forced to fight against. This touched my heart and I figured 'What's the big deal?'"

They divorced after a few years when the student decided to marry his own childhood sweetheart.

She married a fourth time to a "con man" named Dereck who introduced her to his gay lover.

At some point, Andrea did give birth to a third child but put the baby up for adoption in 1961.

ACTING CAREER

In her mid-20s, Andrea got a few acting gigs, landing parts in M*A*S*H, Bewitched and the Russ Meyer T&A classic Beyond the Valley of the Dolls. She would be credited under the name of Samantha

Scott but would also use pseudonyms of Donna Duzzit, Sarah Stunning, and Prudence Smythe.

"She had been a bit player in a lot of TV shows and movies," Riverside County prosecutor James Hawkins said. "She had some beautiful photographs of herself. Facial, bathing suit, different costumes. She was in plays, movies."

Andrea got roles in some late 1960s "nudie cuties" like Horny Hobo, Wild Gypsies, Nude Django and Bad Girls for the Boys. She did manage two get a two episode run as "Betty" in the show Bewitched which would be the high water mark for her in Hollywood.

"She really couldn't make it as an actress," crime author Diane Fanning said. "So she ended up working as a call girl to make money."

Andrea had been thrown off a horse while filming a b-movie. She injured her back and claimed that this forced her into prostitution.

HIGH-PRICED CALL GIRL & DRUGS

"I was finally dating!" she said recalling her decision to become a call-girl. "I had read all Harold Robbins' books to learn about men and a lot of my dreams did come true through with these 'pay dates.'"

According to her probation report, Andrea began using marijuana in her late twenties and used until 1980. She also indulged in barbiturates and morphine based pain medication after she injured her back in the fall of the horse. During her time as a call-girl, she would use cocaine.

MORE MEN

In March of 1980, she married another man after a whirlwind ten-day courtship. The marriage did not last two weeks as her husband went into a jealous rage. Andrea was able to fend him off with a butcher knife, chasing him out of their Los Angeles apartment.

"Andrea was an exceptionally beautiful woman," forensic psychologist Oscar Newsome said. "I mean absolutely beautiful. She knew how to use her body and looks and words to seduce men and get them to do things for her. She was in several relationships and marriages, all short and quick."

DESPERATION TIME

Now in her late 30s, Andrea knew her days as a high-priced call girl would be numbered. She had to meet a "sugar daddy" and fast.

Enter lumber magnate Robert Sand, who at 69 years old was 30 years Andrea's senior.

"Robert Sand had been a lumberman in the northeast," Hawkins said. "He made a fortune there. Retired to Los Angeles. He also had a long standing history with prostitutes."

Sand had been confined to a wheelchair for years. He suffered from multiple sclerosis and was confined to a wheelchair.

Sand had married his first wife Frances in 1939 but they would divorce in 1947. Five years later, they would remarry. She first found out about her husband's proclivities for prostitutes in 1973 which effectively ended their sexual relationship but not the marriage.

"His wife was divorcing him because he had an $800 a week prostitute habit," Fanning said. "And she was just not comfortable with that and she leaves him. So that's how Andrea comes in Bob Sands life."

By December of 1980, Sand had finalized his divorce with Frances. Then he began living with Andrea.

The rich businessman found the sexy former actress and model irresistible. He booked her for repeated engagements as Andrea gave him sex and massages.

"It got to the point where it got so expensive that his accountant recommended that he stopped spending money on her each month and marry her," Hawkins said. "To save money."

"There was the sizable age difference, of course," forensic psychologist Oscar Newsome said. "And the two were introduced by Andrea's 'madam'. So obviously we're not talking the ideal marriage here. It is an arrangement at best."

The madam informed Andrea that Sand sometimes "played rough" but treated the women he sent to her well "in general."

Andrea's fourth divorce became final in December of 1980 and she then moved into Sand's apartment in Westwood where he asked for her hand in marriage. Andrea said "yes" and they moved to a condo at The Springs in Rancho Mirage.

"They lived in a big, gorgeous home," Fanning said. "In a very wealthy area in Rancho Mirage."

"Rancho Mirage is where a lot of political figures, CEOs, and actress and actors retire," Hawkins said. "Its known as the playground of the presidents."

RESPECTABILITY

Sand provided Andrea what she always wanted, respectability and security. They had famous people in their neighborhood like Tammy Faye Baker. So in the beginning, Andrea enjoyed herself.

She wheeled Robert around in his wheelchair as he watched her play golf and tennis. He took her shopping and she would continue to give him therapeutic massages.

"She did have a power over men," Hawkins said. "She had a way about her. She was very sensual. And she would, for lack of a better term, suck you in."

"Andrea Claire was pushing 40 years old," Newsome said. "She had to have seen the writing on the wall when it came to her stripping and call girl days. She wanted the easy life. The rich life. So when she came across Robert Sand she put her best foot forward. Here was a guy, stuck in a wheelchair and had literally money to burn. Most importantly, she knew that he had multiple sclerosis which would only get worse as time went on. She saw him as an opportunity. Marry the old man, wait until he becomes invalid or dies off then enjoy the benefits of his wealth."

CONTROL FREAK

Robert limited Andrea's social life, however. He was a sexual voyeur and made Andrea pose nude for photograph sessions and walk around their condo naked.

"Robert was an old man confined in a wheelchair," Newsome said. "So like most men in that position, he did not want any kind of competition for Andrea. So he kept her confined to the house. They wouldn't go out to eat. He wouldn't let her out, period. She rebelled, of course, but he really want her to be his on-call sex toy."

According to Andrea, Robert liked to spank her with a paddle and masturbated while he watched her have sex with other men. Andrea claimed that Robert became more and more demanding with his requests and fantasies. Every day the envelope was pushed further and further.

"I think her life would drastically change due to a marital contract that we found," Hawkins said. "She agreed to perform sexual services for him. There was a whole list of them. Some of them somewhat perverted. And he would follow her around and photograph her doing everything."

Robert's demands would be increasingly kinky as the months wore on.

"According to Andrea," Fanning said. "Bob got more and more sexually demanding. And the sex that he wanted was more and more sadistic."

MUTUAL ABUSE?

Robert would have complaints of his own, however. He informed his attorney friend that Andrea would routinely berate and insult him as well as leave him alone for long periods as she went off to "play tennis" and that she had a "terrible temper."

"Sand would complain that Andrea would be abusive," Newsome said. "It is unclear whether or not she would initiate the fights with him or she was responding to his own increasing demands. What is clear is that he got more than he bargained for when he married her as he didn't expect her to fight back or display such a temper."

Robert Sand, however, was not going to throw away a Rolls Royce just because it had a few dents in it.

"But he was also compelled to stay with her because she had the most incredible body he'd ever seen," Hawkins said. "And the sex was wonderful."

POISON THE OLD MAN?

With the arrangement becoming more and more intolerable, Andrea contacted a friend and asked him about the effects of Seconal. She said she had already tried to poison Robert and that it didn't work. She also told her tennis partner that her husband would soon die from multiple sclerosis. Her friend said that multiple sclerosis would not kill her husband, Andrea said, "No. He knows he's going to die very soon."

"Andrea had been a sexual plaything all of her life since the age of 15," Newsome said. "She saw Sand as her only way out and yet this was not going to be as easy as she thought. She began to feel resentful at first then it turned into outright hatred. The sexual games that he made her play, paddle boarding, sadomasochism. For even the most hardened prostitute, it all became too much for her."

"That may have been the straw that broke the camel's back," Hawkins said.

Andrea had enough. She wanted a marriage of convenience from a rapidly dying old man. Instead, she got nightly sexual humiliations from wheelchair bound pervert who didn't want a wife. He wanted a sex slave.

"She thought it would be a life of luxury," Hawkins said. "Instead it was a life of somewhat sexual slavery and she just couldn't stand it anymore. Even though Mr. Sand was in a wheelchair I think he was a very demanding person and he exorcised control over her primarily financially."

THE ATTACK

One night in May of 1981 it all came to a head.

Bob Sand laid on the bed, screaming at Andrea to come into the room and perform her sexual duties.

Andrea, however, had something else in mind.

"That's when she attacked him with the knife," Fanning said.

"It was an out of control frenzy," Hawkins said. "Just stabbing over and over and over again. He was stabbed over 27 times and importantly he was stabbed in the heart and severed the aorta."

"The attack was 'overkill' as one psychiatrist at the time described it," Newsome said. "She stabbed the man over twenty-seven times so this was a hate-filled, raging attack of someone who had a high amount of pent-up anger. All the rage and frustration Andrea felt at the humiliation she suffered, hell, maybe all of the rage she suffered for her whole life bubbled to the surface the moment she started stabbing Robert. And she didn't stop there. She picked up a wooden board that she used for exercise and slammed it down on his head so hard that it caused a fracture."

On May 14th, 1981 at 4 o'clock in the morning, security guards at The Springs investigated an alarm coming from the Sands' address. They found the front door open and were soon greeted by an upset Andrea in a black robe. She told the guards that there was a male intruder in the home and he had run out of the sliding glass door in the living room.

She led the guards into the bedroom where they saw the bloodied, nude body of Robert Sand.

Forty-five minutes later, Sheriff's Detective Fred Lastar arrived and the scene was secured. Andrea repeated the story of the intruder and she was allowed to go visit a neighbor.

Investigators would later establish that Sand had been stabbed 27 times and had been hit over the head several times with a 1' x 4' exercise board. There was in fact a trail of blood from the bedroom to the living room's sliding glass door but they found only a single bloodstain on the patio.

There were no footprints on the grass where Andrea said the intruder escaped.

Lastar also found it odd that in the master bathroom above the toilet there was a wet-t-shirt poster of Andrea with her nipples visible under the thin material.

Andrea would tell the Sheriff that she had taken some sleeping pills and had gone to bed early the previous night. She had heard her husband screaming for help and when she investigated she saw one or two men running out of the house.

"She said she heard her husband yelling out," Hawkins said. "She went down the hallway to his bedroom, she saw some stranger in the dark who bumped into her, pushed her out of the way and ran out of the condominium. She went in there to find Robert on the ground."

She looked and saw that Robert was dead. Oddly, she went and washed her clothes when they had gotten bloodied after she tried to help her husband. Even more strangely, Andrea then went back to sleep for two hours before calling security.

"The problem with Andrea's plan was that not only was she a bad actress," Newsome said. "She was a lousy screenwriter. She came up with this half-cocked story of intruders breaking in and stabbing her husband. Sand is a well-to-do retiree. The intruder takes nothing and leaves the buxom actress all alone to sort things through. Right away, the Sheriffs doubted her story. She implored for them to go out looking for the intruder but they found no signs of forced entry. Nothing that would indicate that a stranger had entered their home for the sole purpose of killing a rich old man in a wheelchair."

No weapon was found in the condo but after a re-examination of the place the police found a four-inch kitchen knife under the couch. The autopsy would reveal that the knife was the murder weapon. When this was revealed to Andrea she went and "prayed" and then would declare that she took the knife out of Sand's chest. She claimed she washed both the knife and her clothes.

Laster then asked Andrea if she were willing to take a lie detector test and she refused. At this point, he considered her to be the prime suspect.

The attack on Sand was brutal. The autopsy revealed that the fatal wounds had been to his aorta. He displayed defensive wounds on his arms and wounds which meant that he had been conscious and trying to ward off the attack. The autopsy physician surmised that Sand had been lying down when the attack took place.

PSYCHOTHERAPY

Andrea consulted with her therapist, Dr. Morton Kurland, and he told her to stop talking to the police and get an attorney. He recommended Gary Scherotter, considered the best criminal attorney in Palm Springs.

Andrea heeded his advice despite the fact it was quickly looking like she was a black widow on the prowl for a rich husband to kill.

A TURN FOR THE BIZARRE

On July 23rd, the Indio Sheriff's department received an emergency call from Andrea Sand's residence.

When police arrived they found Andrea nude on the kitchen floor. Her hands and feet were tied behind her and a knife was stuck in her buttocks.

She told the police that she had returned home after a visit to New Jersey. She stated that two men and a woman had tied her up and repeatedly raped her.

During the rape, the intruders informed her that they had murdered her husband and would be back for more.

"The police came into her home," Fanning said. "She was bound hand and foot. And she had a knife sticking out of her buttocks."

"We never found any evidence of the assault," Hawkins said. "We couldn't find any physical evidence on her."

Detective Chris Brown realized that the rope had been tied with slipknots and there was the possibility that Andrea had tied herself up. During an interview with Andrea, Brown stated that he doubted Andrea's story.

"If you don't believe me, why don't you arrest me?" Andrea challenged.

"It's possible you'll be arrested," Brown said. "Based on my past experience, one of three things is going to happen. You'll either kill yourself, kill someone else, or I'll have another call back here for another phony situation."

MORE "ATTACKS"

Andrea began calling the sheriffs on a regular basis, stating that the same intruders came and raped her again.

"She continued to tell us that the intruders returned, kidnapped and sexually assaulted her repeatedly. There were so many incidents."

She also produced numerous threatening letters which she claimed were from the gang of murderers/rapists.

The letters were determined to be fakes as the only fingerprints on the paper belonged to Andrea herself.

"I've been on the bench for fifteen years," Hawkins said. "And I haven't seen any cases as bizarre as this one.

"In all of her alleged attacks," Newsome said. "Andrea was always the victim. There was never any physical evidence or signs of forced entry. These were phantom intruders. She was tested for DNA and they found nothing. So the police knew that they were dealing with someone who was either schizophrenic or making the lamest attempt to throw them off her trail. Amazing that she had so little foresight into what she was doing. Like a bad screenwriter, she had no one to bounce her bizarre ideas off of so she ended up doing a lot of bizarre things that only tightened the noose around her own neck."

FINDING A NEW MAN

True to the pattern of her life, Andrea could not go long without a new man by her side. She would meet Joe Mack Mims at a Christmas party at the Evangelical Free Church. Mims was 56 years old, widowed and a water pump consultant.

Andrea had a neighbor who encouraged her to "find Jesus" and she came into the church of Mims who was a regular attendee of the services there.

Mims became enamored with Andrea and believed her stories about the murder of her ex-husband and the repeated attacks. He went so far as to visit the Deputy D.A. Jim Hawkins and complained that if they knew anything about police work they "would probably have the murderer by now."

Mims then informed Hawkins that he was going to marry Andrea. Hawkins advised Mims against this, stating that they were going to charge her with the murder of Sand.

"Go ahead and charge her," Mims replied. "I'm still going to marry her."

"He became irate," Hawkins said. "He suggested that I spend my time trying to find the intruders that keep returning and assaulting her. And stop harassing her."

"Mims had a classic case of 'Captain Save-A-Ho,'" Newsome said. "Here was this woman who has worked as a call-girl, has two children, has been married five times and he is naïve enough to believe that after listening to a few sermons she is a changed woman. So he becomes her savior, marches down to the police station to intimidate them, marches down to the D. A's office. All the while, Andrea is not saying a word. She has a new man to do her bidding, to plead her case. She's damn good at finding these kind of men. She had been doing it her whole life."

FIRST DEGREE MURDER CHARGES

On March 25th, 1982, Andrea's attorney Gary Scherotter was notified by the D.A.'s office that Andrea would be charged with first degree murder. Scherotter sent her to the court where she posted $100,000 bail and was set free.

The next day, Andrea and Joe Mims were married.

SIXTH TIME IS A CHARM?

Andrea did not want to sell the condo at The Springs until Sand's estate was settled. Mims sold his own home and moved in with Andrea at The Springs.

"He took it upon himself to try and protect her from the return of the intruders who kept kidnapping and assaulting her," Hawkins said.

"Again, the poor guy is smitten by her charms," Newsome said. "Here is a 56-year old man living as an anonymous life as possible. He meets a woman sixteen years his junior. She's stunning, she's posed in Playboy, been in movies and now she is reformed at the church of his choice. He's convinced she's in love with him and is willing to move heaven and earth to make protect that illusion."

MORE BIZARRE STUNTS

Two months later after they were married, however, Mims called the police and informed them that Andrea had been kidnapped. The officers began a search but Andrea returned home on the same day claiming she had been abducted and raped by the same intruders as before.

No physical evidence was found but Mims remained steadfast in his belief that Andrea was telling the truth.

Andrea was able to put on a false front with Mims, appearing to genuinely care about the man as they would engage in social gatherings at church.

But on Halloween of 1982, Andrea convinced Mims that they should take a drive together. They drove along Highway 74 and turned into an isolated dirt road. Andrea threw a bed sheet on the gravel and began to give Mims fellatio.

Mims climaxed into her mouth after which she spit his semen into a tissue. She then told him to roll over on his stomach and she would give him a massage.

"So Joe thinks this is the best thing going," Fanning said

Mims was like putty under her expert hands but then something hit him hard on the back of the head.

He screamed in pain until he was hit again.

Turning around, he saw Andrea holding a hammer, wanting to hit him again. He pushed her off and grabbed her arm, ripping the hammer out of her grip.

"What in the name of God are you doing?" he asked.

"I've got to knock you out so that people will believe I've been raped."

Mims finally saw the light. He knew that she had thought to use the semen in the tissue to provide evidence she had been raped.

"The fact that she tried to kill him (Mims) was a real game changer," Hawkins said. "The evidence that we needed to really go forward on the case."

KNOCKED INTO COMING INTO HIS SENSES

Mims dressed and drove Andrea home before going to the hospital to get his head stitched up.

The next morning, Mims moved out of the condo. He notified authorities of the assault, prompting an attempted murder charge to be added to the first degree case against Andrea.

Mims moved to have his marriage with Andrea annulled. Andrea's bail was then revoked and she went to jail to await the trial.

Andrea's attorney, Gary Scherotter, now believed that she wasn't mentally stable and had the court examine her for competency. Andrea was taken to Riverside General Hospital for observation and tried to commit suicide twice during her stay there by slashing her wrists.

"Her whole world finally came crashing down," Newsome said. "She was completely out of control. A psychologically broken woman with no way out and no answers, she finally broke down and tried to end it all."

MENTALLY COMPETENT

Scherotter would resign as her attorney as the Sand estate had been tied up in litigation and she could no longer afford to pay him. Andrea was appointed a public defender in Charles Stafford who changed Andrea's please from not guilty to not guilty by reason of insanity. His defense lay in the hopes that the jury would believe that Andrea had been driven crazy by the men in her life who abused her and it all came to a blowout when Robert Sand forced her to be the victim in his bizarre, sadomasochistic fantasies.

But the prosecution found a man named Richard Cordine who was a convict serving a twelve year sentence for robbery at a Nevada State Prison. Cordine stated that Andrea had started a pen pal relationship with him in 1977 which continued for years until Joe Mims found out about it and stopped it. Cordine would testify that Andrea called him after the Sand murder and confessed "I stabbed the bastard."

Her prosecutor, Robert Dunn, would call her a "malingerer who would lie to achieve her own end." He dismissed the idea of Andrea killing Sand out of self-defense on the grounds that Robert was a paraplegic.

"She planned Sand's murder to get money from his will," Dunn said. "She received about $150,000 in cash and $100,000 equity in the couple's condominium."

"She stabbed the man twenty-seven times," Newsome said. "This scared the crap out of the jurors. Andrea would take the stand and give the performance of her life by recounting her tales of abuse but in the end, it was those twenty-seven stab wounds that stayed in the mind of the jurors."

After deliberation, a ten-woman, two man jury found Andrea Mims guilty of first degree murder. The judge sentenced her to 26 years to life and sent her to the California Institute for Women in Frontera.

"When the judge read the verdict to her," Fanning said. "She slammed down a box of tissues on the thing (table) and said 'I killed him because he called me a whore!'"

"Manipulation always worked for Andrea," Newsome said. "She knew how to manipulate men all her life. She thought she could manipulate everyone else the same way, cops, jurors, telling them about her tales of abuse and woe and thereby mitigating her own culpability in all the bad things she did.

REMARRIAGE?

Joe Mims tried to jump start his life after Andrea was sentenced but could not seem to get over her. He knew that she had killed Robert Sand but also believed she had been forced to do it as her attorney had claimed. He then heard a radio program discussing PMS and concluded that Andrea had suffered from the condition when she killed her husband and attacked him.

Mims did research on PMS then visited Andrea in prison, telling her of his findings. Andrea requested progesterone from the jailhouse doctor but the physician found no symptoms of PMS. He finally gave in to her demands, however, and the drug seemed to improve her demeanor.

Andrea displayed good behavior in prison. Mims had a renewed hope that he would get a new trial for Andrea on the basis of his PMS theory. He proposed marriage once again and Andrea accepted. He wrote love letters to Andrea such as the one below:

"My Darling Drea,

I promise you a love that will be true, I will always put you first in my life. I will do all I can to meet your every need, while we are apart it will be hard, but our God will bring you home to me. I love you with all my heart,

Your Hubby,

Joe"

On May 13th, 1986, Mims showed up at the prison to marry Andrea. He never made it past the front gate, however, as he began to experience chest pain then collapse. He was transported to to Chino Community Hospital where he was pronounced dead of a heart attack.

After Mims' death, Andrea once again reiterated her story that intruders had killed Robert Sand.

During her prison term she became a prolific artist at the Central California Women's facility and won several awards as well as becoming a Buddhist.

"I'm very proud of my achievements," she said in a prison newsletter. "I've used the past 20 plus years to improve myself, learning to grow in a positive way and also to heal and forgive myself."

Andrea was paroled in 2012 but suffered from ovarian cancer which soon got into her lungs. She would die at the Mesa Verde Convalescent Hospital in Costa Mesa, CA.

"I do understand that she suffered at the hands of men," Hawkins said. "Why she had the relationship problems that she did but I don't think that was ever an excuse to forgive or forget what she did to Robert Sand."

HUSBAND KILLER : THE TRUE STORY OF TRACEY GRISSOM

SARAH CAMDEN

Claiming to be a victim of rape and other abuses, a distraught Tracey Grissom would travel to her ex-husband Hunter's workplace and shoot him six times in the back, receiving a twenty-five-year life sentence for his murder.

Her defense attorney would argue that Tracey was motivated by post-traumatic stress disorder caused by her Hunter's constant abuse and sexual assaults. One jury member had even asked the judge to be lenient in her sentencing as they were not allowed to hear details of her Hunter's alleged abuses (beatings, rape, sodomy).

But what really happened in the years that led up to May 15th, 2012? Was she in fact the victim of years of abuse by a psychotic husband? Or did she want to cash in on his $100,000 life insurance policy?

INSTANT ATTRACTION

The couple would meet during a dinner party in 2003 in Tuscaloosa, Alabama. Tracey was twenty-one years old and going through a divorce. She had a son, James Michael, from the previous marriage.

Family and friends would describe the union as "love at first sight." Hunter was blown away by the young Tracey's blue eyes and facial beauty.

"For him, it was love at first sight," crime author William Phelps said. "She was gorgeous."

A whirlwind courtship would ensue and the couple would elope in 2004.

"In the beginning, it was good," Tracey told CBS' 48 hours. "We had a friendship. Just your normal, honeymoon phase marriage."

"He was fun," Tracey said. "And he was attractive."

Hunter was two years younger than Tracey, however, and his mother felt that he had jumped the gun too early in the relationship.

Her words proved to be prophetic as after only eight months into the marriage, the marriage went south.

According to Tracey, their marital problems began with Hunter's drug addiction.

"I had caught him smoking marijuana," Tracey said. "Doing illegal things could cause a problem and I couldn't risk losing my son over."

Tracey claimed that she threatened her new spouse with a divorce but Hunter gave her his word that he would stop with his drug use. She stated that the relationship improved and the decided to start a construction company together.

"I took out an equity line to start a company," Tracey said. "Which was Grissom Construction. It was all in my name."

Hunter specialized in building elaborate boat docks. He had an artistic eye and could do docks, stairs, and other accouterments. The business began to grow in short order.

"They're going to take on the world," Phelps said. "They're going to be entrepreneurs and they're gonna make it."

They then had a daughter of their own, Anna Grace. The child was a long time coming for the couple. They had been trying for a long time as Tracey had five miscarriages before Anna Grace was born.

"She was premature," Tracey recalled. "Her heart and lungs were not developed. A very stressful time."

Behind closed doors things were rocky. On the surface, however, things looked good. They had a young family and were making money.

"All-American family," Phelps said. "White-picket fence. The whole nine yards. Middle-class. Suburbia. Maybe the Prince Charming that she's been waiting for."

But again, this was only on the surface. Tracey harbored secrets of her own. One of which was her own addiction to prescription drugs.

"Psychologically, there's something going on here," Phelps said. "There's something going on behind those beautiful eyes and it ain't good."

Tracey would often turn on on the children, showing off her temper. Then she would turn on Hunter.

"This would cause friction in the marriage," Phelps said. "And where there's friction, there's fire."

SETTING THE STAGE

Tracey would later state that Hunter would "act strangely" shortly before she filed divorce. She was a registered nurse and gave him an over-the-counter drug test. According to her, Hunter tested posted for marijuana, Oxycontin, opiates, and methamphetamine.

Hunter would later be arrested for marijuana possession but his family would insist that he never did the harder drugs.

Tracey would file for divorce in the summer of 2010 after six years of marriage. According to her, this would prompt physical abuse from Hunter.

Hunter had to move out but their divorce agreement would allow him access to the home.

"In September of 2010," Tracey recalled. "That was the first time he physically hit me. It (the abuse) got progressively worse. He had made the comments that if I told anybody he would kill me. I believed him."

Hunter' co-workers and family members would have a different take on the situation, however. His co-workers remembered a time when she tracked him down at one of the jobs and made a scene.

"She's screaming, jumping on him," Hunter's co-worker said. "Said something about him having another girlfriend and used the expression about, 'You are mine. I'll kill you. I'll kill you. You are mine."

"She's borderline demonic," Hunter's mother said. " mean, I absolutely believe—that she is that troubled."

Hunter's family continued to believe that he did not abuse Tracey.

"He did not have an abusive, an angry bone in his body," Hunter's aunt Gina said. "In fact, we kind of laughed at him because he was too laid-back."

The divorce was finalized in October of 2010.

EVIDENCE OF ABUSE?

Loran Richards was the first of Tracey's friends to notice the minor injuries on her body. She would inquire about the bruises but the answers she received were always evasive. Seeing Tracey with a black eye, however, forced her to try and get more answers.

"I said, Tracey, you may have terrible luck," Richards recalled. "But nobody is so unlucky that they trip, fall down the stairs, and hit their face on a baseball in the eye socket. So don't give me a lame excuse. You don't have to give me any excuse, but let's take a picture."

Tracey broke down. She gave her friend all of the grisly details, detailing the abuse she suffered at the hands of Hunter. Loran then became her advocate, taking pictures of Tracey's injuries. She would later state that she saw blood stains and other signs of abuse at Tracey's home.

THAT FATEFUL NIGHT

Now divorced, Hunter would arrive at Tracey's home on November 22nd, 2010.

According to Tracey, he then became enraged when Tracey told him that she had spent the night with a new lover.

"He told me that he was gonna kill me," Tracey recalled. Tracey stated that she tried to escape, running into the closet in order to "get away from the kids and to pray." Tracey's eleven-year-old son from a previous relationship was in the home as was the four-year-old daughter they have together.

Hunter caught up with her and knocked her to the ground. He tied a belt around her ankles and then began choking her.

Half-conscious, Tracey alleged to have been raped and sodomized.

The brutal attack would leave Tracey unconscious. She would wake up the next morning on the bathroom floor.

"I called Hunter," Tracey recalled. "I told him that I was bleeding and that I was hurt and that I needed help. And he told me, 'Fuck you. I hope you die.'"

Tracey wound up in the emergency room after the attack. Hospital records would show that she had a laceration on her head, bruises, and ligature marks on her feet.

Tracey would then be referred to the Turning Point domestic violence center.

Marian Waters would describe Tracey's injuries as among the worst she had ever seen in a twenty-year career.

Waters would testify that Tracey had suffered a horrific assault. She described her mental state as typical of someone who had just been raped; fearful, jumpy, fearing for her life.

Tracey had suffered a hematoma on her side that was the side of a grapefruit. She also claimed to have experienced rectal nerve damage which would require surgery as well as torn vaginal muscles requiring her to have a hysterectomy.

Police were called and Hunter would be arrested for rape, sodomy, kidnapping and domestic violence.

"And at that point, I feared for my life," Tracey recalled. "And I feared for my children's life."

A HIDDEN AGENDA

Hunter would be freed on bail but Tracey got a restraining order against him. She bought a gun and did not go anywhere unarmed.

She took photos of her injuries on the night of the alleged attack and texted them to Loran. Later, they would take more pictures.

Angered, Hunter would stop paying her spousal and child support. Tracey, however, may have had another scenario in mind for obtaining money.

She had forced Hunter to take out a $103,000 life insurance policy around the time their daughter was born.

On May 24, 2012, the day before Tracey shot Hunter, she would place a call to MetLife that was recorded.

"Thank you for calling MetLife, this is Pam. May I please have your name?"

"Tracey Grissom."

Tracey would then explain that she was angry that her husband stopped making payments on his policy. During their divorce proceedings, he had agreed to continue paying the premiums. Tracey stated she was calling to make sure that they had the correct address on file.

"Is there anything else I can do for you today?

"That's gonna be it!" Tracey said, hanging up.

"Well, May 14th was just like any other day," Tracey said, explaining the call to the insurance company. "However, I had moved four different times. Me and my children were running. We were running from Hunter. So I had called the company to let them know that they had my old address and to make an address change."

FALSE RAPE?

Shelly Standridge was hired by Hunter to defend him in the rape case. She would state that Hunter denied raping or even assaulting Tracey that night. Hunter did, however, admit to the fact that he and his wife had consensual sex that night...Rough consensual sex.

"So that night," Standridge said. "Hunter said that she was depressed and claiming she was going to kill herself. She was saying she wanted their relationship to work."

So she undressed in front of him. Her beauty was always impossible for Hunter to resist.

The two had sex despite Hunter having a new girlfriend at home.

Hunter's aunt, Gina, believed that Tracey wanted to kill Hunter before the rape case went to court.

"He had a new girlfriend, he was living with her," Phelps said. "He was moving on with his life. Hunter would claim that Tracey was jealous, obsessive, even stalked them."

"Hunter had moved on," Hunter's aunt said. "There was some court dates coming up that would prove that Hunter was innocent. There were court dates coming up that he would get visitation to his daughter. She had a lot to lose."

Tracey was on the anti-anxiety drug Klonopin. Hunter would tell his attorney that Tracey would take more than her prescribed dose. Because of this, she fell and cut her head. Hunter would then leave the house around 10:30 pm and go to his father's house. Tracey would call him hours later, at 3:20 am.

Hunter would state that Tracey had called to threaten him. She told him if he didn't want the responsibility of the children then she would make it where he would never be able to see them again.

Hunter's attorney did not know what Tracey's motive was for crying rape. She was very upset that he had a girlfriend.

MORE LIES...

Hunter would be arrested nearly twelve hours later, to his total shock.

Tracey would give her side of the story to the police which later is proven to be false.

She would tell police that Hunter had thrown her against the bathtub around 10 pm and claim to be unconscious until 4 am the next morning.

"But her phone records show she was on the phone all night, so she was never unconscious," Standridge said. "She was also using her data at 10:42 that night. She was using it again at 10:50 that night. ... She sends a text to her boyfriend at 1:49 am. She sends a text to her friend at 2:07 am. She sends another text to her boyfriend at 2:07 am."

Tracey would blame the calls on Hunter.

"All I do know is I was not the only person using my phone that night," Tracey said, suggesting that Hunter used her phone.

Medical records would show that Tracey's head wound was "purely superficial".

Only one suture was needed.

Furthermore, there was nothing on the medical record to support the fact that Tracey experienced vaginal and rectal tears. She did have bruises on her ankle and legs but the photos taken by police at the emergency room would not resemble the same photos that Tracey and her friend Loran would take days later. In the photos taken at the emergency room, an area of Tracey's body has no bruises. Days later, there is discoloration.

Tracey's attorney would blame the discrepancy on "blood thinners" which would cause Tracey to bruise easily.

There was also a discrepancy in her phone records. She would take a photo of her inner thigh, a deep bruise. This area of her body was not photographed by police during her emergency room visit. But on December 9th, almost two weeks later, Tracey took a photo of her inner thigh with the deep bruise

"He (Hunter) told me that he would make it to where nobody would ever want me," Tracey said after a 2010 attack. "I didn't report it because I thought he would kill me."

THE FINAL STRAW

Tracey woke up pissed on May 15th, 2012.

Hunter had been ordered to pay $2,100 a month for the rest of his life. He was not complying with the court order claiming that he was "out of work."

Tracey stated that she was on her way to a job interview when she saw a Grissom Construction sign out of the corner of her eye.

She stated that her initial plan was to take a photograph of Hunter at the job site in order to show proof that he was working as part of her litigation.

"I was getting ready to take the picture and when I looked up he was standing almost directly towards the front of the boat trailer," Tracey said. "He was looking back directly at me. He had this face, that's like mean - just, I don't know how to describe it. I mean, I see it over and over like it's right there all the time. He flipped me the bird, which to me was kinda like, 'Yeah I'm workin. Screw you.' And at that point, I panicked. At that point, I didn't know what else to do except to defend myself."

Tracey started firing. The first shot hit Hunter in the arm. He started to run and she fired again repeatedly. One of the bullets punctured Hunter's heart and he died of massive internal bleeding.

William Dockery was working with Hunter and was an eyewitness to the shooting. Hunter had turned to Dockery before the shooting and told him to "call the law". Before Dockery could pick up his cell phone, Tracey had commenced shooting.

Tracey then pulled out her own cell phone and called the cops on herself. She tearfully described that she had just murdered her husband.

CONFESSION

Tracey told detectives exactly what was going through her mind when she came upon Hunter at the construction site.

"Tell me about what happened," the detective said. "What led up to...what's going on."

"In November of 2010, he beat me unconscious and raped me...and, and left me for dead....and, and I finally pressed charges against him and he told me that he would make my life a living hell...and that's what he's done."

"What, what happened this morning that led up to you going..."

"I was going to work and I saw him...and he's been claiming that he-he's not working. And, so I pulled in there to take a picture of him...cause it was the truck that's still in my name...and the boat that's still in my name...and the trailer that's still in my name...He just stared at me and flipped me off...and I just went in there and shot him...I just shot him, I shot him, and I shot him."

Tracey would be distraught and tearful during her interrogation room confession. A few weeks later, however, she would call the insurance company to let them know that Hunter had died.

"Well, I was actually calling because I didn't know what I needed to do ... Hunter passed away May 15th and I actually am going a court case right now because it was due to self-defense..."

Hunter's family went ballistic over this. Tracey would claim that she had no money but she continued to pay his life insurance premiums.

"Even through the times when she's screamin' that she's destitute and has no money ... she continued to pay life insurance premium," Hunter's mother said.

"I don't think my sister concocted a story," Tracey's sister said. "Just so she could get insurance money. ... But that's all they (the prosecution) had."

THE TRIAL

Tracey's allegations of rape and sodomy would not be allowed in court testimony. She was allowed, however, to detail the effects of Hunter's abuse on her were.

Taking the stand, Tracey would lift up her shirt in court and show herself wearing a colostomy bag. She stated that she had undergone several surgeries after her husband's daily rapes wherein she suffered permanent rectal and vaginal damage.

Hunter's family was then allowed to speak at the hearing.

"This tremendous loss has changed me," Hunter's mother, Melanie Garner said. "And I don't know how to change back."

Chloe, Hunter's sister, had a victim's services officer read her letter in court.

"Tracey is psychotic," Chloe wrote. "She is the most selfish person human being on this earth."

"Every mother should pray every night that your son doesn't fall in love with someone like Tracey," Hunter's aunt, Gina Grissom said. "There have been lots of allegations against Hunter. We've never believed anything that has come out of her (Tracey's) mouth."

His aunt then looked directly at Tracey.

"Hunter was proud of his name. Why would you still choose to use our name, and bring it down?" suggesting that if Tracey hated him so much why didn't she go revert to her maiden name after the divorce.

The jurors would find Tracey guilty of murder. She would be sentenced to twenty-five years in prison.

One of the jurors, Janice Kelly, would contact Grissom's attorney Warren Freeman the morning after the trial. She had remorse over her decision and said that she wouldn't have convicted her had they had the rapes and abuse allegations been introduced as evidence.

"I feel I made a mistake," Kelly said. "If I had to do it over again, we'd have had a hung jury. We didn't get her side. She did not get a fair trial."

"We voted to convict because there was no dispute that Tracey shot Hunter," the jury foreman wrote in a letter that was addressed in the courthouse. "Jurors didn't believe prosecutor claims that she did it in order to collect a life insurance policy. We felt the shooting was a crime of passion, not for financial gain and that she should be sentenced accordingly. I wish we had seen evidence of the rape allegation. We feel that she just 'lost it.'"

"It's not fair, it's not fair!" Tracey sobbed as she was led out of the courthouse and to jail.

"We think the sentencing was too harsh," Tracey's attorney Warren Freeman said. "Considering you have the foreperson of the jury actually saying, we don't feel like she should be punished according to being found guilty of murder. Let's just say that there will be a basis for a new trial, and part of it will be something that the jurors saw that they weren't supposed to see and I'm going to just leave it at that until I file my motion."

"My son died running for his life," Hunter's mother said. "I don't know what was running through his mind but I hear him say 'momma.'"

"People who think that I murdered him in cold blood," Tracey said. "Either don't know the whole story or don't know everything that's happened.

Tracey was asked on CBS' 48 hours if she regretted pulling the trigger on that fateful day.

"No," she said flatly. "Because if I hadn't I would be dead. I truly believe that."

"She has a way of making everything she does look right," Hunter's aunt, Gina scoffed.

LISA MONTGOMERY

174

WENDY TITTLE

Lisa Montgomery would meet Bobbie Joe Stinnett in an on-line chatroom called "Ratter Chatter" under the pretext that she wanted to purchase a rat terrier puppy from her.

But what she really wanted from the pregnant Bobbie Joe was her baby.

Lisa would arrive at the Stinnett home and strangle the young woman into unconscious before cutting out the baby from her stomach with a kitchen knife.

She would then show case the baby around her small town, introducing her as "Abigail."

Investigative authorities would find out that Lisa would suffer from what psychiatrists called "pseudocyemesis." A psychological delusion where the subject believes she is pregnant.

The gruesome crime would shock the town of Skidmore, Missouri with its population of only 300 people. Once a community where they could keep their doors unlocked at night, the townsfolk would never be the same.

BOBBIE JOE STINNETT

Bobbie Joe had lived in the small town of Skidmore, Missouri all of her life. She was a shy but happy cheerleader in high school and graduated with honors of May of 2000.

"She was intelligent and fun-loving," Bobbie Jo's mother Becky Harper said. "She never knew a stranger."

Three years after graduating, Bobbi Joe would marry her childhood sweetheart in Zeb Stinnett. The couple would tie the knot on April 26th, 2003.

"She was real quiet," Zeb said. "She pretty well kept to herself. I was the same way. I guess that's why we clicked so well."

Bobbie Joe would work at the Earl May Garden Center which served as both a pet store and plant nursery. Zeb worked in production at Kawasaki manufacturing. Later, Bobbie Joe would join Zeb at the plant and together they were saving money to buy their first home.

To make money on the side, Bobbie Joe was also a champion breeder of rat terriers. She ran the side business with her husband and they deemed the business "Happy Haven Farms.

"Our puppies are placed in only the very best homes with the family that fits them best," the website read. "Let us help you find your next pet, rat terrier or otherwise."

Bobbie Joe would also engage in on-line forums that discussed rat terriers. She would often be the go-to person to chat with because of her expertise in the genetics of breeding.

It was here in this on-line chat room she would meet "Darlene Fischer". Fischer was accused of misrepresenting her dog's pedigree by other members in the forum but Bobbie Jo would defend her.

Little did she know that Fischer was doing more than misrepresenting her dog's breed.

She was misrepresenting herself.

Darlene Fischer was really Lisa Montgomery.

"(Lisa) told us all she was pregnant with twins," chat room member Nancy Strudle said. "And about a month and a half ago her messages were 'I lost one of the twins. It's so terrible, but they saved one twin.' We didn't believe she was pregnant. I don't know how she fooled her family and community."

Bobbie Joe had met "Darlene" at a dog show in Abilene, Kansas in November of 2003. A few years later, "Darlene" would again touch base with Bobbie Joe via the Internet message boards of her rat terrier site.

"I was recommended to you," Lisa Montgomery wrote under her pseudonym. "And have been unable to reach you by either phone or email. Please get in touch with me soon as we are considering the purchase of one of your puppies and would like to ask you a few questions."

Bobbie Joe would e-mail Lisa back and the two would arrange a meeting.

Later that afternoon Bobbie Jo received a call from her mother, Becky. Her mother wanted her to come pick her up from her job at Sumy Oil. Bobbie Jo stated that she couldn't as she was waiting on a customer to come look at the puppies. At that moment, Lisa's red Toyota Corolla parked outside.

"There they are," Bobbie Jo said. "I've got to go."

It would be the last time they would ever speak.

LISA MONTGOMERY

Lisa Montgomery's life was troubled from the beginning. It was alleged that she was sexually abused by a stepfather as well as emotionally abused by her own mother.

John Patterson, Lisa's biological father, would express regret when he abandoned his daughters to their mother.

Lisa's mother, Judy Shaughnessy, wanted out of the marriage but John didn't fight for custody of the children as he was an alcoholic at the time.

"(I made a mistake) leaving my two daughters with that crazy lady."

Lisa's half-sister, Diane Mattingly, would agree with Patterson in that their mother was no angel.

"It was like walking on egg shells," Mattingly recalled. "You could never please her. If you did something wrong, you got hit."

"Lisa was raised in an abusive home," forensic psychiatrist Paula Orange said. "But she did not have any violent tendencies in her background. She was a well-versed liar and probably used this as a way of coping with an out of control, angry mother. So she developed a lot of negative coping mechanisms. This doesn't excuse her behavior but it does give us an idea of where she was coming from."

After Patterson left the family, Denise would be put up for adoption as their mother told them that it was their fault that he left.

"(Lisa) was clinging to me. I was her mother in reality," Mattingly said. "I was the one who protected them. I was the one who took care of them."

These early traumatic episodes would be the catalyst for the adult mental illnesses of Lisa. She would become obsessed with pregnancies and develop a lifelong habit of never telling the truth about anything.

Carl Boman, who was both the ex-husband and stepbrother of Lisa, would state that Montgomery saw pregnancy as a way to get attention. The couple would have three daughters and a son in less than four years. She would then get a tubal ligation without any forethought as doctors warned her against having more babies.

But Lisa would cheat on Carl during their tumultuous fourteen-year marriage. She would move from her native Oklahoma to New Mexico and then settle in Kansas.

"She was selfish," Boman said."A chronic liar with low self-esteem and critical of others. But she didn't have the potential for violence."

Lisa would pretend to be pregnant with Carl a few times during their marriage. Carl would file for divorce in 1993 but in 1994 they would reconcile and remarry. Why? Because Carl thought she was pregnant and didn't want to leave the baby abandoned.

Four years later, however, Lisa would file for divorce. She took their four children and moved in with Kevin Montgomery. Kevin had three kids of his own and they formed a "Brady Bunch" style union in his home of Melvern, Kansas.

Kevin was a quiet guy, an electrician by trade while Lisa was a housewife. She talked only of herself or her children, spending her days raising goats for wool. She would teach all of the children how to weave, dye and spin the yarn. But neighbors would describe all of the children as unkempt and dirty as when she wasn't weaving wool she was "vegging out on the couch."

Still, one of her older daughters remembers their time together fondly. Lisa would make old-fashioned dresses and bonnets with her daughters before they would attend fall festivals. She also encouraged one of her daughters to play football on the boy's team, going so far as addressing the school board to make it happen.

She would marry Kevin two years into their living arrangement as Lisa would claim to be pregnant. She began walking around the house in maternity clothes and announce a due date of December. She told everyone who would listen about her pregnancy, including Pastor Mike Wheatly.

The pastor told Lisa that she was "kind of small to be having a baby that soon."

"I've always had small babies," Lisa said, he didn't pursue the topic any further.

Kevin, who worked at a sign company over seventy miles away from their home, firmly believed that Lisa was pregnant.

"It was impossible for Lisa Montgomery to have another child," crime writer William Phelps said. "Her tubes were not tied. Her tubes were burned, cauterized. Which is an irreversible process. How could a husband sleep next to his wife of nine months and not know that she's pregnant? How could he look at her when she got out of the shower and not know he was pregnant? Didn't he go to any of the doctor's appointments? Lisa Montgomery manipulated this guy to believe that she was pregnant."

Meanwhile, former husband and step-brother Carl worried about his children under Lisa's care. He filed for sole custody which would force Lisa to admit in court that she was not pregnant. Carl knew Lisa's game. Once the judge saw Lisa's mental delusion first hand it would be easy for him to win custody.

Still, Lisa was adamant about playing the pregnancy card.

"She begins to buy diapers," Phelps said. "She begins to buy baby items. She tells the town, the husband, the children, everyone around her is pregnant. She lied through her childhood. Her teen years, her adult life. One of the lies she perpetrated was I'm pregnant. Lisa would say 'I'm pregnant, I'm pregnant, I'm pregnant' but then she would cover the lie with 'I miscarried.'"

"She begins to wear baggy clothes. She begins to make doctor's appointments. Fake doctors' appointments. She begins to swallow air when people are around. She begins to do all these things knowing that when the ninth month comes he's not going to have a baby."

This time, however, Lisa really needed a baby.

Lisa would go into grocery stores and shopping malls looking for a baby. She approached one woman holding an infant in a grocery store aisle.

"God, what a beautiful baby," Lisa said to the young mother.

"Thank you."

"I can hold her for you," Lisa offered. "You can do your shopping. She'll be safe with me."

The young woman was taken aback by Lisa's offer and overall demeanor. She politely excused herself and headed out of the store.

But Lisa still needed a baby.

"Lisa had a creepy vibe about her," Orange said. "She was more than awkward, she had a rat-like appearance with her hang-dog face and black-rimmed glasses. She would look down at the floor when she would talk to someone and gave off a vibe of an inbred Annie. Bobbie Joe, however, was not the judgmental type. So when the two met, Bobbie Joe wouldn't let any kind of street sense take over. She would want to be fair and non-judgmental."

Surfing around on the Internet, Lisa would visit her favorite on-line chatroom called "Ratter Chatter", a dog breeding forum dedicated to rat terriers.

Clicking through the pages, she sees pictures of Bobbie Joe and the puppies.

"The one thing she notices about Bobbie Joe," Phelps said. "Is that Bobbie Joe is pregnant."

"I think she looked at Bobbie Joe as being an incubator," Boman said.

Montgomery would use the pseudonym "Darlene Fischer" and wrote to Stinnett that she was pregnant also. Making every effort to befriend Bobbie Joe, the two women chatting via Instant Messenger and had conversations about their pregnancies. Montgomery then informed Stinnett that she wanted to buy a dog from her and arranged a meeting at her home.

"Lisa Montgomery is communicating with Bobbi Jo Stinnet online," Phelps said. "She's someone who enjoys these types of dogs that Bobbie Joe raises. Makes a date with Bobbie Joe to look at some puppies. But inside Lisa's car she has a knife, a rope, and a home birthing kit."

Thinking Lisa arrived at her home to look at the puppies, Bobbie Joe lets the woman inside without a second thought.

"Lisa Montgomery looks at the puppies," Phelps said. "She asks Bobbie Joe to bend down to pick up the puppy. She took out the rope, put it around her neck and choked her out."

Bobbie Joe did struggle with Lisa as some of her assailant's blonde hair was found in her fist, indicating that she had pulled out some of Montgomery's hair before she was subdued.

Lisa then cut the premature infant out of Bobbie Joe's stomach, slicing her open laterally with the kitchen knife.

"The evidence to me shows that she regained consciousness while the incision was being made, a struggle ensued and she was strangled again," Dr. Mary Case said. The 23-year old Bobbie Joe would fight desperately against the 39-year old Montgomery. But her attacker had the kitchen knife.

Lisa would slice across Bobbie Jo's body in a furious assault, cutting up her hands, face, and elbows. She would inflict eight jagged slices across Bobbie Jo's stomach.

Dr. Case believed that Bobbi Joe struggled upright because there was a large amount of blood found on the bottom of her feet. So she was either standing or sitting with her knees raised when Montgomery sliced her open. This could not have been possible had she been unconscious.

Lisa then removed the baby and cut the umbilical cord. Initially, it was thought that Bobbie Joe was murdered by someone who had someone medical skill.

"I think that maybe it's not as complicated as it might seem," Sheriff Graves said. "I'm not a medical expert, but I think anyone with a reasonable amount of skill could probably accomplish this."

Now with a newborn infant in her hands, Lisa could prove all of her doubters wrong.

She had a baby of her own.

Bobbie Joe would be found by her mother, Becky. She came into the Stinnett home and found her daughter laying in a pool of blood.

Becky would call 911.

"It looks like her stomach had exploded!" she said in her harrowing phone call.

"The images that are in your head are horrible," Boman said. "The idea of what happened. I mean it still effects me. I was allowed to see evidence and pictures and stuff and it's terrible."

Paramedic attempts at trying to revive Bobbie Joe would prove to be unsuccessful.

She was pronounced dead at St. Francis Hospital in Maryville, Missouri.

Lisa traveled along an isolated back road with her kidnapped baby. At some point, she either found a watering hole or stepped into a fast food restaurant to wash the baby down. She then

She then sealed her belly button with a pair of clips, giving herself the appearance of someone who just left the hospital. Lisa then called her husband Kevin. She told him she had gone shopping in Topeka, went into labor and had given birth.

Her husband was surprised but pleased by the news.

Her pastor, Mike Wheatly, was next on the call list. Lisa and her family had attended his church for the past four years. Wheatly was again, surprised at the revelation and stated that he looked forward to seeing the newborn.

Kevin and their high-school-age children then got into their car and drove to Topeka. They would meet Lisa in the parking lot of a Long John Silver's restaurant. They would show off "Abigail" in the restaurant to other customers.

Kevin, Lisa, and the stolen newborn would drove home in his pick-up. Their teenage children would drive home in Lisa's car, a red Toyota Corolla.

They brought the baby to see Pastor Mike Wheatly and he expressed surprise that there actually was a baby. "I was doubtful that she was pregnant in the first place," Wheatly said.

But both the pastor and his wife took turns holding Abigail for about an hour's visit. The church couple did,however, think it was odd that a newborn baby should be out doing the rounds so soon.

Police did not rule out anyone in the murder of Bobbie Joe Stinnett. Initially, they would question Zeb but the husband had an airtight alibi. He was at work.

They would issue an Amber Alert for the baby and could only hope that the infant was still alive.

Authorities would catch a break almost immediately, however. An alert dog breeder from North Carolina would inform the FBI of Stinnett's exchanges with "Darlene". She sent the links over to the FBI which read as follows:

"Darlene, I've emailed you with the directions so we can meet," Bobbie Jo wrote. " I do so hope that the email reaches you. Great chatting with you on messenger. And do look forward to chatting with you tomorrow a.m...talk to you soon Darlene!"

Computer investigators then contacted internet providers who were able to trace the fictitious e-mailer to Montgomery's home which was over 130 miles away.

Police then began surveillance of the home and spotted Lisa with the newborn baby. A "dirty, red pinkish, two door vehicle" was reported being seen outside Stinnett's home by a neighbor and the same vehicle matched that description outside Montgomery's home.

A dirty and dusty red Toyota Corolla.

Authorities would arrest Lisa and save the baby who was immediately taken to the hospital.

Lisa double-downed on her lies when interrogated by police. She told them she had delivered the baby herself only a day earlier. They checked with the Topeka women's clinic where Lisa claimed to have delivered Abigail only to find out that they had no babies born there on the day that Lisa claimed.

Lisa would then succumb to the pressure and confess to the killing and kidnapping.

"She confessed to having strangled Stinnett and removing the fetus," the local sheriff said. "Lisa Montgomery further admitted the baby she had was Stinnett's baby and that she had lied to her husband about giving birth to a child."

Bobbie Joe's baby would be brought to the Neonatal Intensive Care Unit at Topeka Hospital. Zeb would later describe his daughter as "a miracle."

The gruesome murder would stun the residents of Skidmore, Missouri. A small town with just over 300 people, things like that never happened there.

"It's very hard for me to accept this," Nodaway County Sheriff Ben Espey said. "Nobody here could ever perceive this taking place—to have a fetus taken out of someone's womb and then doing an Amber Alert to try to find a child."

. "We felt betrayed. We were angry," Pastor Mike Wheatly said. "But most of all, we're very, very, very sad."

The crime would resonate in the dog breeding community where Bobbie Jo Stinnett was so popular as well.

"I am sitting here in shock, not knowing how to break this," a user named Teresa wrote. "I just received a phone call from a reporter in Missouri saying that Bobbie was killed today and her fetus stolen! I am absolutely horrified!"

"I cannot believe how sorrowful I am," a chatroom user named Jill wrote. "They have taken Lisa into custody. I don't know what is worse—the horrible crime—or the possibility that it might be Lisa. Someone just shoot me."

Lisa would be charged with "kidnapping resulting in death." Her husband Kevin would not be charged as authorities believed that he knew nothing of Lisa's intent or act of murder.

"My heart ain't broke just for me and Lisa and her kids," Kevin Montgomery said. "It is them (the Stinnett family) too. That was a precious baby. I know."

During a pre-trial hearing, a neuropsychologist would state that the head injuries that Montgomery suffered a few years ago could have damaged a part of her brain which controls aggression. Her attorneys would also argue that Montgomery also suffered from pseudocyesis, a delusion that she was pregnant.

A second neuroscientist would dovetail this assertion, stating that Montgomery's childhood sexual abuse and post-traumatic stress disorder made her susceptible to pseudocyesis.

Prosecuting attorney Roseann Ketchmark dismissed the theories, however, calling them "voodoo science."

Famed forensic psychiatrist Park Dietz would testify for the prosecution. He had been the expert psychiatrist for other high-profile cases such as Jeffrey Dahmer, the Unabomber, Andrea Yates and Susan Smith.

Dietz would testify that Montgomery did not suffer from pseudocyesis and discounted the theory as "outrageous."

Jurors found Montgomery's excuses "outrageous" and would find her guilty of murder on October 22nd, 2007. She was given a death sentence and in April 2008 a judge upheld the decision.

Her case US Supreme Court who denied Montgomery's petition to be removed from death row.

Lisa Montgomery is now being held at Federal Medical Center, Carswell in Fort Worth, Texas.

She is in line to become the third woman to be put to death by the federal government since 1927 and the first in over fifty years.

Lisa's oldest daughter would move in with friends while her youngest child would move out of state. The two middle children would live with her ex-husband and step-brother, Carl.

At Bobbie Jo's funeral, her husband Zeb would read the 23rd Psalm beside her casket. The Reverend Herald Hamon of Skidmore Christian Church, the same man who married Bobbie Jo and Zeb, would deliver her eulogy.

Bobbie Jo would be the third member of her family to have been murdered in the early 2000s. She had a cousin that was stomped to death by her boyfriend as well as having another cousin who disappeared.

"Abigail" has been renamed and lives with her father.

PSYCHO CHICK : THE TRUE STORY OF PENNY BJORKLAND

DARLA PUGH

Eighteen-year-old Rosemarie "Penny" Bjorkland woke up in a bad mood on February 1st, 1959. Her first thoughts upon awakening were "today is the day I will kill someone."

Penny showered, got dressed and went for a walk through the hills of San Francisco clutching a .38 caliber pistol. She would reach an isolated spot and practice her new hobby.

Shooting guns.

Only on that day she would not be satisfied shooting empty beer bottles. She wanted to shoot a human.

Penny Bjorkland did not look the part of a thrill killer. A freckle-faced teenager with blonde hair, blue eyes and ponytail, she looked normal at first glance. Her parents were church-going people and her three brothers (ages 9-13 at the time) had no troubled history at all. By all accounts, her upbringing was one of normality and comfort even though she hated her mother. During her teenage years, the following scenario would play out every Sunday morning:

"Let's go!" her mother would yell from outside her bedroom.

"I don't want to," Penny said.

Her mother barged into her room, dressed to the nines. Penny had her best dress on but was laying on the bed, immovable.

"You're getting your dress wrinkled!"

"I hate church," Penny said.

"You have to go," her mother said. "It is that simple. Let's go! Let's go now, Penny!"

Penny would remain frozen in bed.

Her participation at school was no better. Her classmates always thought there was something "off" about her. She kept to herself and was a loner with no close friends.

"Her mental illness went undiagnosed," forensic psychologist Paula Orange said. "She had a hard time determining what was real and what wasn't. She could keep a false front of a person who seemed 'normal' on the surface so that is why she was able to avoid any kind of psychiatric evaluation. She never did anything beyond what the average rebellious teen was doing at the time. There wasn't one big action that set off alarm bells."

Penny did have a nervous vibe about her, showing jittery body language and biting her nails every minute. Her biggest infraction in school was being caught with a "screwdriver" mixture, a mug of Vodka and orange juice. She would cut school often and eventually drop out before taking a job as a typist.

With bizarre flights of fancy ricocheting through her, Penny was still able to maintain appearances. She would wear the most fashionable clothes and have the latest hair style. But while her peers would be talking about Bobby Darin and Elvis Presley, Penny's fantasies would be much darker. She would earn a reputation at school for doing and saying strange things. On one occasion, she approached two of her classmates who were eating their lunch outside. Carrying a shoe box, she asked if they wanted to know what she had hidden inside.

The two young women shrugged their shoulders, more interested in what they were going to wear for the prom then what Penny had in her little box.

"You don't know what's inside my shoe box," Penny teased.

"I don't know Penny," one of the young women said, deciding to humor the strange girl. "What's inside your shoe box."

With dramatic effect, Penny opened up the box to reveal a long blade.

"What are you going to do with that, Penny?"

Penny just giggled, closed the box, and walked away.

"I just remember her as being crazy," Darlene Norry Ferguson recalled. A former schoolmate of Penny, her recollections of the woman who would kill her husband remain etched in her memory forever. "She was just strange. How many girls take a shoe box with a knife in it to school on a regular basis?"

The shoe box revelation aside, Penny did not look or seem threatening. Just weird.

"She was a strange person," Darlene said. "And we stayed away from her."

"Penny liked to do off the wall things to gauge people's reactions," Orange said. "She was testing the waters, so to speak. Showing a knife to a bunch of girls, she would giggle at how they would respond. The response would inevitably be fear and shock. It was part of the fun for her, she enjoyed freaking people out. It was a game to her."

But on February 1st, 1959, she graduated from merely shocking people to murdering them.

"Her fantasies turned into an obsession," Orange said. "For whatever reason, she began obsessing on what it would be like to shoot someone. People would see her walking down the hallway with her finger pointed like a gun. People like Penny fantasize to escape. But in Penny's case, it is hard to fathom what she was trying to escape from. Her parents were relatively normal and it isn't uncommon for a teenager to not want to go to church. She does not fit any psychological profile of any killer I have studied. There is no traumatic event in her past which would serve as the catalyst for her violent behavior. No physical abuse, no sexual abuse. No mental abuse aside from the fact that her mother wanted her to come to church with the rest of the family. There is absolutely nothing in her psychological profile to suggest that she would become a murderer."

On that fateful afternoon in February, Penny would take to the hills for more target practice. She liked the feel of the gun in her hands, the power, and control. Having the hot pistol in her hands made her fantasies seem all the more real. She could finally follow through. She could imagine what how a killing would feel like but her fantasies could only go so far.

She wanted the real thing.

Dressed like a young woman on her way to an ice cream social, Penny walked down the trails. She tucked the revolver in the waistband of her stretch pants with thoughts of menace dancing in her head. Would she feel guilt or shame if she killed someone? Who would it be? Who would be the unlucky victim of her violent fantasy?

She knew she wanted to kill someone. The real question was who.

Then she heard tires on gravel closing in behind her. Turning around, she saw a pickup truck inching up the trail.

She recognized the man inside.

August Norry.

It was a typical day for the twenty-eight-year-old August Norry. He was dumping lawn clippings in the San Bruno Mountains, enjoying the cool afternoon.

"Augie" was mustachioed and darkly handsome. Athletic, he played minor league baseball, trying out for the Pacific League's San Francisco Seals where his father was a coach. He was a decent pitcher but failed in his tryout so he turned to ballroom dance instruction with Arthur Murray. Seeking a change, Augie then decided to go into the Army. He suffered wounds in the Korean War but returned home and used G.I. Bill money to go back to school. He worked two jobs with a full-time landscaping gig at the Lake Merced Country Club as well as being the gardener at a chemical plant in nearby San Leandro on weekends.

"He was the type that if we didn't have enough money he went out and got another job," Darlene said. "He said 'if we don't have enough money. I'll go make more."

He had been married for a year and a half to Darlene with a baby on the way, unknown to both of them.

"Augie was a very happy, jovial, friendly man," Darlene recalled. "Very good natured, patient. Just really a wonderful man."

Things were looking up for August "Augie" Norry.

Until he saw Penny Bjorkland walking down the trail. Blonde with her hair pulled back in a ponytail, she was young. Eighteen or nineteen, maybe. She was full-figured but had a cute face. It was uncommon for a pretty young woman to be walking by herself. The hills were relatively safe but it was an isolated place. If something bad were to happen, there would be no witnesses. A veritable ladies man, he had met Penny twice before and told her he was single. They met when she was walking around the Crocker estate and they would later have lunch together at a drive-in cheeseburger joint. She had given him his number but he didn't call back.

"Hi there," Augie said, watching a smirk creep across the attractive young woman's face.

"Hi," Penny said, inhaling from her cigarette and blowing the smoke out.

"That's a steep climb you're looking at," Augie pointed at the incline of the trail up ahead. "You need a lift?"

"Sure," Penny said.

Norry reached over and unlocked the door for the young woman, not knowing what she had in store for him.

They drove deeper into the hills, the cheerful Augie eager for small talk.

"What are you doing way out here?" he asked.

"Target practice."

"Target practice?"

Penny took out the gun from her waistband. Augie was immediately taken aback.

"What are you doing with that?"

Penny loved the look on the man's face. The same look of shock and surprise that she got when she would show the girls at school her long knife.

"You up for a little target practice?" Penny asked.

"I just got back from Korea," Augie said. "I've had too much damn target practice."

Without warning, Penny pointed the gun out of the passenger side window and began to shoot.

"The hell you doing?"

"Like I said," Penny giggled. "Target practice."

"You stupid fool," Augie yelled. "You need to knock that off! Didn't you hear me? I was in Korea! Got shot up. Guns are nothing to play around with like you're doing."

"Did you shoot anyone?"

"I've seen people get shot up."

"What was it like?" Penny asked, her eyes beaming with curiosity.

Augie looked at her strange. "You don't want to know."

The gardener came to a stop near a tree. He needed to get this nut out of his car.

"I do want to know," Penny said pointing the gun at Augie. "I have to know."

Without warning, Penny shot Norry in the chest.

"You stupid bitch!" Augie yelled. "The hell are you-"

Penny continued to fire, shooting Augie several more times until the gun clicked empty.

Penny continued to fire, shooting Augie several more times until the gun clicked empty. Her adrenaline flowing, she got out of the car and picked out took out more bullets that she had hidden in her pack of cigarettes. Reloaded, she fired five more shots into Augie.

Augie offered no resistance. He went into shock from the first bullet then slumped into his seat, dead.

Penny got out of the car and fired five shots into the man.

Augie offered no resistance. He went into shock then slumped into his seat dead, from the multiple wounds.

Penny stared at her victim with a crazed look in her eye. She waited for a moment, feeling nothing that a normal person would. No guilt, no shame. Just pure adrenaline. Relief.

She then ran around to the driver side, putting more bullets into the chamber. Penny shot Norry five more times. Not satisfied, she walked back over to the passenger side and reloaded before shooting Norry again.

The forensic evidence would reveal that Norry was shot while sitting in the driver seat of the car. Some blood was found on the inside of the door which would indicate the door was open when he was shot. He may have been trying to escape.

"The fact that August Norry was driving along at the same time that Penny was looking for someone to kill is an extreme fluke," Orange said. "As the cliche goes, the wrong place at the wrong time."

Penny got back into the car and drove for fifty yards, barreling over a barbed wire fence and before stopping the car again. She pulled Norry out of the vehicle and propped him face up on the ground. She shot him again, emptying the chamber.

She would shoot Augie a total of eighteen times. Fourteen of the bullets were lodged in his body; three in the head, three in the neck, three in the chest, two in the stomach and the rest in his arms and legs.

"Penny shot Augie in every part of his body," Orange said "It was like she was conducting her own science experiment, watching as each bullet entered his flesh and gauging the reaction. She either liked the feeling or was waiting for some epiphany to come to her as she fired away. She had no motivation other than the fact that it was something she had been fantasizing about for so long. She pumped bullet after bullet into Augie, over and over again."

Penny got back into the vehicle and drove away.

GETTING RID OF THE EVIDENCE

Norry's car was covered in bullet holes and blood, it looked like a mafia hit. Police recovered the vehicle at the end of a lover's lane on Christmas Tree Hill later that night. In the back seat of the car, they found a book with the title "The First Year of Life."

Norry's body would be found the next day by a passersby.

There was a boy who saw Penny drive away in Augie's truck, speeding down the road like a bat out of hell. He informed the police about the woman, saying she was swerving around the road and almost hit him.

Penny then went home and had dinner with her family. The next day, she threw both the gun and her left over bullets down a storm drain in San Francisco as she went to work. Over the following weeks, she would monitor the newspapers and clip articles that talked about the unsolved murder of August Norry. Cutting the news briefs out with meticulous precision, she placed them in a shoe box for safe keeping.

"The fact that she was taking clippings out of the newspaper bespeaks to a kind of wannabe celebrity mindset," Orange said. "No one paid much attention to Penny at school as she was a loner or what not. By shooting Augie, she achieved a certain status that she wanted and had a desire to mark the moment by taking out the clippings."

Police were taken aback by the overkill of the murder. They chalked it up to a crime of passion, believing the blonde woman that the little boy saw in the vehicle was a lover of Norry.

"We have to remember that police during this time period always looked for motive," Orange said. "So they believed that either the wife did the crime, a jealous girlfriend or a jealous boyfriend of a lover. The brutality of the crime was so over the top that it had to be something personal. The motive of killing someone, just for the sake of killing them had not entered into the investigators' psyche just yet. So, unfairly, they began looking at Norry's wife."

The police then brutally interrogated Darlene Norry, August's wife. They ransacked her home, not believing her story of innocence. Norry was a ladies' man and his co-workers at the Lake Merced Country Club suspected that he was cheating on his wife. Other than that, they found nothing after questioning Norry's family and friends. He was a good citizen; a hard-working and reliable man trying to provide for his family.

Police had nothing for two months. They would interrogate numerous blonde women who lived in the area near Norry to no avail.

These interrogations would accomplish nothing except scare the living crap out of the women who just happened to fit a profile of being young, blonde and living near August Norry.

The police had only the boy who saw the woman and a blood-stained rhinestone necklace. But the ballistic report on the bullets used would prove to be the link they would need. They discovered that the bullets were known as "wadcutters", specifically designed for target practice. They had a blunt tip and were used by gun aficionados who liked to reload and practice.

San Mateo Sheriff Department detectives William Ridenour and Milt Minehan were able to trace the manufacturer of the bullet mold to a company in New Jersey. They lucked out in that only 10,000 were sold and they were able to find out which Bay Area gun shops had purchase orders on the unusual bullets. The detectives then visited the gun stores one by one. One thing led to another and they were eventually led to a twenty-three-year-old mechanic named Lawrence Schultze. They took samples from Schulte's bullets and compared them to those used on Norry, coming up with a perfect match.

The detectives then took Schultze in for questioning.

"What happened to those bullets you have?"

"They were stolen."

"Stolen?"

Schultze would continue to try and give the detectives the runaround but eventually his lying caught up with him. The police finally got him to give up a name of a woman.

"I sold a box of fifty wad cutters to Penny."

"Penny?"

"Penny Bjorkland. She tagged along when my girlfriend and I went to the hills. We did some shooting."

The description Schultze provided met criteria the police were looking for. Penny was young, blonde and liked to shoot guns in the hills.

The next morning, police arrived at Penny's home, waiting for her to come home from work.

They found Penny's family to be a normal, working-class household. She had straight-laced parents and three brothers who had raised eyebrows at the fact that Penny would be in some kind of trouble with the law.

Detectives Ridenour and Minehan were a bit taken aback when Penny got home. They found the attractive, freckle-faced young woman to be outside the box of what they expected a thrill-killer to look like. Her facial expression betrayed no emotion as the police asked permission to search her room.

It was there that they found newspaper clippings of Norry's murder.

The police took Penny in for questioning but she remained steadfast in her innocence. Police took her to a local restaurant instead of downtown to the station. Treating Penny with strawberry shortcake, they finally got her to confess to the shooting in the wee hours of the morning. Penny was then driven to the scene of the crime where she re-enacted the events for the police and reporters.

"I stepped out of the vehicle and shot him four times," Penny said performing for both the police and a cameraman who filmed her acting out the murder. "Then I took his body out of the car and laid him out. Then I shot him some more. Bang! Bang! Bang! Bang!"

The newspapers reported that Penny had giggled like a teenager going to a high school dance as she detailed how she killed Norry. This could have been exaggerated for effect, but the news story sold like hot cakes. The story went nationwide with a full page spread in the local San Francisco Chronicle. One reporter described Penny as being "pretty and plump". A normal, teenaged girl who just happened to have shot a man she didn't know eighteen times. The police would state that

Penny did not react as if she had just taken someone's life. August Norry meant nothing to her, a non-person that she used to fulfill her fantasy of killing someone.

"I felt better mentally," Penny said, describing her feelings after she committed the crime. "Like it was a great burden lifted off of me. I have no bad memories about it. I always wanted to see if I could do something like this and not have it bother me."

"She talked as if there was this great burden lifted off her," Orange said. "'I finally did it,' she said to herself. Because of her bizarre psychology and lack of an abuse history, it is hard to gauge if she would have gone on to become a serial killer. My guess is that she would have continued on unabated. There would have been long gaps in which she would have been fine but eventually she would have become addicted to the rush, addicted to the killing like most serial killers do. Although she did not have the same abusive background of a stereotypical serial killer she had the same lack of empathy. The same lack of feeling for another human being."

The revelation of guilt left police scratching her head. Penny stated that she wanted to plead guilty and even the district attorney was taken aback by Penny's lack of remorse.

"I did it," Penny said. "There is no use going through a trial. I did it. I wanted to know how it felt to shoot someone. To satisfy my curiosity. So I did it, its over and you can take me to jail now."

Penny said that she did not know that Norry was married and felt bad that his wife was now a widow. She felt nothing for Norry.

Police and psychologists remained dumbfounded. Penny looked and talked like a normal human being. Her co-workers painted a different picture, describing her as a loner who would shun others at her job at the Periodical Publishers Service Bureau in San Francisco. She was also known to carry a knife around in the office.

Penny refused any kind of psychiatric evaluation. She did tell one policewoman that she held hatred for her parents because "they made her go to church."

Despite that revelation, her parents sought desperately to defend their daughter, going so far as to mortgage their home to pay for an attorney.

"They had nothing to do with it," Penny said with cold indifference. "I guess this does affect them, but that's not my concern."

Penny's parents would hire Joseph Murray but even he could not believe her indifferent mindset and unwillingness to alter the slightest details in the story to help her cause. Numerous psychiatrists were called in to speak with Penny and they all said the same thing.

"There's nothing wrong with her."

"If we had to absolutely choose a motive, we could say that Penny did all of this to shame her mother," Orange said. "Penny was a discipline problem and her mother was a devout, religious type. But again, that kind of dynamic happens all across America. For her to just go out and shoot someone at random makes her case a head scratcher."

"For about a year and a half I've had the urge to kill someone," Penny said, her tone one of shame. "I'll admit that the motive sounds crazy, but I wanted to know if a person could commit a crime like this and not worry about the police looking for her or have it on her conscience. I've felt better since I killed him."

During the trial, Penny did not seem to grasp the severity of the circumstances. She giggled inappropriately throughout the proceedings, alternating between laughing and looking bored.

Penny would plead guilty to Second Degree Murder. She would get a lesser sentence because the crime was not premeditated but purely random.

South San Francisco Municipal Judge Charles Becker would sentence her to life in prison with eligibility for parole in seven years.

"I am unhappy," she said after her verdict was read.

"But Penny got off light, to say the least," Orange said. "The judge viewed the crime as random and not premeditated. But had they listened to Penny talk they would have realized that this was premeditated the moment she got a hold of that gun. She had planned the attack the moment she awoke that morning."

August's wife, Darlene, would give birth to his daughter two months after the verdict. The police had angered her so much that she moved further north to have her baby in peace. She could not believe that both she and her family were brutally interrogated by the police when they already had Penny as a suspect.

"They were around to insult me just before they caught her," Darlene said. "That is the reason I had to get away for a while."

"I found out about one month after he was murdered that I was pregnant. I remember when I had Cindy (her daughter) and I was in the hospital and there was this woman with me and she was all upset because her husband wasn't there at that moment. And I kept thinking 'well, at least he's gonna come.' So that was probably the hardest thing for me was when I had the baby."

Penny Bjorkland would be released from the California State Prison for Women at Corona seven years after her sentencing.

Her whereabouts are currently unknown. She would be seventy-five years old at the time of this writing.

www.ingramcontent.com/pod-product-compliance
Lightning Source LLC
Chambersburg PA
CBHW021435150726
47989CB00001B/258